ZARATHUS

ZARATHUSHTRA

THE TRANSCENDENTAL VISION

P. D. MEHTA

FOREWORD BY
PROFESSOR NOEL KING

ELEMENT BOOKS

© P. D. Mehta 1985
First published in Great Britain by
Element Books Limited
Longmead, Shaftesbury, Dorset

ISBN 0 906540 68 2

Printed by Billings, Hylton Road, Worcester

Designed by Humphrey Stone
Cartography by Denys Baker

Contents

Contents

Contents

Preface

Words and thoughts are only symbols of the Truth. Just as a photograph is not the living person but may help us to recognize that person when we meet him, so words and thoughts may help us to become clearly conscious of Truth. And just as we can know a living body as it really is only when it is stripped of all coverings, so can we be clearly conscious of Truth only when all the covering words and thoughts about it are absent – when we are completely silent.

The writer sees, and the perceptive reader will understand, that no finality attaches to word or thought, spoken or written, by anyone, be he prophet or peasant. There is no end to the movement of coming upon the Truth and, with progressive development in course of time, of its expression in more lucid and inspiring terms. The actual Vision is one; its interpretations innumerable, often conflicting and confusing. Terrible tragedy has always resulted when fanatics of one faith have claimed finality for their own particular expression of Truth and have clashed in cruel conflict with devotees of another faith.

The compassionate, wise man eschews finality. He rests quietly in a tranquil, intensely alert state of open-minded, constant investigation; for he knows that Truth is ever virginal to the innocent mind of the innocuous man.

Just as it needs an expert jeweller to evaluate a gem correctly, even so only a person who has experienced at least a touch of Transcendence – and has carefully observed its effects in his own life – may attempt to present the founder of a world-religion and his teachings. The writer makes no claims for himself; he has only tried to convey what has become clear to him of the Vision granted by Life. If the reader, after calm and honest consideration, can respond to the expression – and not merely agree or disagree with it – he may realize freedom from fear and anxiety, dejection and sorrow. Self-reliant by virtue of such freedom, he can be a light and a blessing to a world in pressing need of Renovation.

Acknowledgements

My grateful thanks are due to Mrs. Susan Harris for typing the manuscript; to Mr. Denys Baker for the drawing of the map and the Zarathushtrian emblem; to Element Books for their care in the preparation of the book; and to my sister, Mrs. Avabai B. Wadia, for reading the manuscript and for her helpful comments and encouragement.

It is never easy to free the powerfully-conditioned mind from ancient, deeply-venerated, but now outworn and obstructive, religious beliefs – so tenaciously held by millions and so rigidly imposed by the merciless authority of ecclesiastical orthodoxy. Whoso earnestly aspires to realize the freedom of the spirit must invariably go – and go entirely alone and unprotected, except by the Truth – 'into the desert'. It costs a lifetime of intellectual travail and emotional distress in the Silent Void before one is met by this freedom and given the strength to live by it.

But help comes, in rare, and ripe moments, seemingly from nowhere, but actually from the Now-Here, through one's brother-man though he may be quite unaware that he is the helper. With hindsight, he who is helped knows the helper. My deeply grateful thanks are due to two whose sympathetic understanding and supportive encouragement made it possible for this book to see the light of day. My expressed as well as my inexpressible thanks to John H. Moore, and to Professor Noel King whose strong and gentle Foreword tells all that needed telling.

P.D.M.
London, March 1985

Foreword

Human tongue falters in any attempt to describe the glory, the tragedy and the achievement of those we in the West call 'the Zoroastrians'.* We can but contemplate their past and present, recalling disjointedly a few reminders of their greatness.

The Zoroastrians have handed down scriptures which, among the revealed living religions, are perhaps the oldest in the world continuously in use. Their literature is correspondingly among the most venerable in any Indo-European tongue. Ideas associated with Zoroastrianism affected the dynasty of Cyrus in ways not easy to define but we know that Cyrus was called 'my friend' by Jehovah himself. His successors brought together, in considerable freedom and through self-development, an empire which stretched from the Indus to the Nile.

The westward spread of the Zoroastrians' civilizing influence was unfortunately stopped at Marathon. They stood in the firing line to receive the pyromania of Alexander (so-called 'The Great'). A little less than a millennium later, they received the frantic on-rush of the newly-Islamized Arab hordes. In due time, the poor survivors stood against the devastations of the Mongols. Yet these same Zoroastrians influenced the basic thinking of Judaism, Mahayana Buddhism, Christianity and Islam; that is to say, they have affected the psyche of over half the human race.

In India, Zoroastrians fleeing from Iran were received 'as sugar in a full glass of water', as the Gujrati legend puts it; the place was full, but they took up no room and imparted sweetness. During the past two centuries, their descendants

*Zaroaster is the Greek form of the Avestan form Zarathushtra.

– now called Parsees – have emerged as an Asian community ready to assimilate modernization, industrialization, technology, science and business management. A major criterion by which one may measure the beneficial effect of different religious influences is gained through observing the quality of the average community member as encountered in the ordinary affairs of life over a period of time. By this criterion, the follower of the teachings of Zoroaster scores highly – whether one meets such a person in Tehran, the desert of Yazd, Bombay, Nairobi, London, Melbourne or Toronto. There is evident in him or her an inner strength, tranquillity, balance, integrity, and indeed joy, which few others achieve in such measure.

If it is not easy to speak sufficiently of Zoroastrian quality, it is also difficult to speak adequately of Phiroz Mehta, the author of this book. He is a member of the community by descent and by initiation and is further qualified to speak of Zoroaster through life-long study of the teachings, through meditation and much more besides. He grew up in Sri Lanka and daily observed the oldest of surviving forms of Buddhism. He knows the Pali canon well, has close acquaintance with living Hinduism and considerable knowledge of the Vedas and Upanishads. And he also has deep appreciation and understanding of Christianity.

Since it first appeared in 1956 I have used Phiroz Mehta's *Early Indian Religious Thought* with my students in Comparative Religion in West and East Africa, India and, since 1968, in the U.S.A. His second book, *The Heart of Religion* (lovingly called 'THOR' by us) has been a god-send to my Californian students; they find that the books not only assist their academic needs but inspire their own thinking also. This present book brings us again the same clarity of thought, lucidity of vocabulary and strength of style. Again we see thought put together with careful analysis, strict logic and absolute rationality. Yet there is a lyrical beauty and a warmth and love coming from humanity at its highest level. Here is a teacher who gets away from the guru or high professional level, who like Sakyamuni asks the learner – be he or she at university, in the home or in the street – to think for himself or herself, to reject anything that does not stand to reason. He does not destroy miracle, myth and faith; he shows a humankind-come-of-age how to understand and make their own the age-old vehicles of knowledge, gnosis and wisdom. The true teacher stands before us, patient, loving and enabling.

This work makes a signal contribution to Zoroastrian studies, one which in meaning and understanding far surpasses the products of the university academic factories. But beyond this, the author gives in outline his basic and mature thinking on God, the Universe and Humankind. It is a line of thought of great importance in the development of late twentieth century thought. This outline stands out so clearly in these following pages but it is not easy for someone else to state it succintly. I will try.

Since the days of Darwin and Newman there has been a continuing discussion on evolution, 'development', the relation of religion and science, the nature and future of God, the cosmos and humanity. Sri Aurobindo, Teilhard de Chardin and Bonhoeffer contributed. Then, in recent years, world-renowned experts like Sir Alister Hardy, Dr. Thomas Torrance and Seyyid Hossein Nasr have spoken. Phiroz Mehta – thoroughly at home in the worlds of science and music as well as world religion, a citizen of both East and West, an experienced teacher and explainer, a 'popularizer' in the best sense – asks the human race to attain its full adult stature and to take off to that fully humane and divine status which is ours by right.

It is my privilege and duty as writer of this Foreword to state why I think this book to be outstanding. It abounds in original thinking but, for me, after forty adult years immersed in the study and teaching of comparative religion, there are four points made which are especially demanding

– demanding that we should take them up and take them further. (I mainly use here a cento and *catena* of what follows in the book.

1. Truth is ageless and immutable; but its temporal and temporary trappings must be discerned and recognized for what they are. In every age, we finite beings, to the best of our highly-limited and fallible capacity, try to formulate the truth in words. But what may be a vital form for one generation can be a stumbling block for a later one. A great deal of our inherited thinking about the divine, the human being, heaven and hell falls into this category.

2. The human being ordinarily functions in the context of the finite and temporal but can find a transcendent culmination in unitary holistic consciousness with its associated power to function in the infinite and eternal – as exemplified by the Perfected Holy Ones.

3. Immortality, properly understood, is to be experienced whilst embodied.

4. The importance of understanding the meaning of *asha* (Virtue) for the living of the pure and holy life, the heart of religion in daily practice.

I commend this study to you knowing that it is of the greatest importance.

NOEL Q. KING
Professor of History and Comparative Religion
University of California
Santa Cruz, 1985

Abbreviations used in text

AV	Ardāg Virāz Nāmaz
BU	Brihad-Āranyaka Upanishad
CU	Chāndogya Upanishad
Dd	Dādistān-i dinik
Dk	Dinkard
ed	edition or edited by
GBd	Greater Bundahishn
Mkh	Menukh-i Khrat
Rev	book of Revelation, New Testament
RV	Rig-veda
Vd	Vendidad
Ys	Yasna
Yt	Yasht

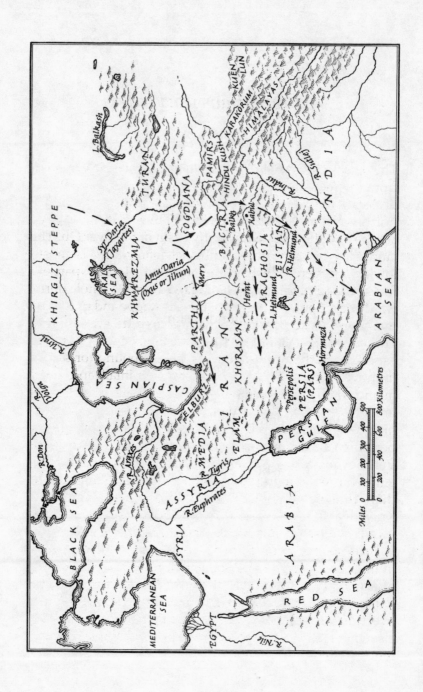

1

The Background

The 9,000-mile belt of high mountain and plateau extending from the Aegean Sea to the Bering Straits cuts the continent of Asia into two distinct, strongly-contrasted sections. The north-western section contains Turkestan, the Khirgiz steppe and the forested, marshy basin of the river Ob. This land bloc of some three million square miles is mostly lowland, covered towards the north by a large expanse of forest giving place to mountain flora along its whole north-ward edge. South of the forest there is steppe and grassland, merging into steppe-desert with a large desert core over Turkestan. The Ob and the other great Siberian rivers, especially in their lower courses, are ice-bound for several months of the year. There is scanty rainfall and much inland drainage. The absence of sea influences, due to the immensity of the continent, makes this Arcto-Atlantic hinterland an almost uninhabited region. Prevailing temperatures add to the discomfort of those who live there. Verkhoyansk, just beyond the Arctic Circle, experiences temperatures ranging from 90°F to −94°F – a range greater than that between ice and boiling water! Tomsk and Krasnoyarsk have typical winter temperatures of −2°F and −12°F, whilst Yakutsk, further north, reaches −46°F.

Thus no great settlement of people could take place of old in interior Asia. The inhospitable northern steppe, devoid of a granary of economic strength, housed only pastoral nomads whose hardiness and mobility enabled them to overrun, though not overwhelm, prosperous civilizations elsewhere. So their impact tended on the whole towards renovation rather than destruction.

South of the immense arc from the Aegean Sea to the Bering Straits lie Arabia and the Fertile Crescent, Iran and Afghanistan, Pakistan and India, Burma, Malaysia and Indonesia, China and Japan. Barring the desert tracts in Arabia and Iran, these lands are well watered by the melting snows of the highest and most massive mountain systems in the world. Radiating from the Pamir plateau, there are the Himalayas, Hindu Kush, Karakorams, Kuen Luns and Tian Shans whose melting snows feed the Indus, Sutlej, Ganges, Brahmaputra, Irrawaddy, Salween, Mekong, Si-kiang, Yangtze-kiang and Hoang-Ho – rivers which are the life-blood of vast agricultural populations.

Two words of significance in connection with Zara-thushtra and his teachings are agriculture and renovation.

About 2500 BC, the steppe folk of the north-western bloc tamed the horse, a native of the snowy slopes between Mongolia and Siberia. They took him, harnessed to the plough of south-west Asian origin, into many lands, thus making themselves a dominating influence in the history of civilization. In the second millennium BC, the smelting of iron developed, probably among or near the Hittites of Anatolia. The copper dagger became the dirk. The horse-men evolved the sword, first made of bronze, later of iron. Warrior herdsmen, equipped with horse and sword, driven southwards because their ancient northern home had become ice-bound – and still further by locusts, by hostile tribes and by drought – split into two main groups in the course of time. One went to Haroyu (Herat) and spread afterwards to Iran, and the other went to Kabul and thence to the Panjab. (Afghanistan in those days was Eastern Iran.)

The location of the original homeland of these warrior herdsmen – the tall, haughty, virile, fair-skinned Aryan-speaking Indo-Europeans whose irruption into history was marked by cruel destructiveness, followed later on by spiritual and material progress and renovation – is still a matter of investigation and argument after more than a century of research. It seems as if their homeland may have been the Ukraine up to the Caspian Sea, or the stretch of steppe east of the Caspian. Perhaps both these regions provided them with their roaming space. Their original language, now unknown, was the source of Vedic and classical Sanskrit, Avestan, Greek, Latin, Keltic and the Teutonic and Slavic languages.

Some Indo-European societies practised agriculture and raised cattle. They were patriarchal. Their military organization was designed for expansion by conquest*.

The causes of separation of the hitherto undivided Aryans were probably their different ways of life – either peaceful settlement based on subsistence agriculture or raiding and enslaving others. Which was to be the more effective? Associated with this problem was the question of religion.

The Indo-Europeans had their own theology and a developed sacrificial ritual. They knew the curious compulsive effect on their own psyche of chanting. So they thought that if the ritual were chanted by a properly trained celebrant, the god – to whom the praise and supplication were addressed – was bound to respond. Even in our own day, nations in conflict pray to God (the same God!) to grant victory to their own side (which is always good and just, whereas the enemy is always evil and unjust!).

Within the ranks of the undivided Aryans arose those whose growing sensitivity to Unitary Wholeness inclined them towards monotheism; the rest remained worshippers of many gods (*devas*). The former, getting tired of nomadic wandering, tended to become the settled agriculturists; the latter tended to be the ones who raided settlements and gathered booty. The success of these marauding *deva*-worshippers was attributed to the magical power of the *mantras* (spells) of the Soma sacrifice and the intoxicating

*Note the Indian doctrine of *mandala* expounded in Kautilya's *Arthashastra*.

enthusiasm produced by the Soma drink; it was as if the god Indra himself led the attacks.

When it became necessary for the settled agriculturists to make a complete break, the *deva* religion of the hateful marauders was branded as evil, as the source of all misfortune. It was supplanted by the Ahura religion of the agriculturists. This development started well before the birth of Spitama Zarathushtra. But it was not possible initially to produce a totally different religion. Spitama's predecessors worshipped several good spirits, *ahuras* – Lords of Life or the Living Ones.

The term *ahura* is the Avestan counterpart of the Vedic *asura*. In Zarathushtrianism it has always stood for the supreme spirit. In the oldest parts of the Rig-veda it stood for the supreme spirit, God. In the sense of deity, it was applied to the chief deities – such as Varuna, Agni, Indra, etc., who were good spirits – but no more so than the gods (or goddesses) of the Greek Olympians.

The significance of this is that all gods represent the natural forces of the universe which are dualistic – positive and negative, constructive and destructive, pleasant and painful. In actuality they are neutral (like neutrons, each of which is composed of a positive proton and a negative electron). They function one way or its opposite according to the nature of the prevailing circumstance, in obedience to Divine Law – Asha, Rita, the Will of God (the moral Will, not a capricious will). Later on, the term *asura* came to mean the very reverse of its original meaning. The *asuras* became the demons, the enemies of the gods. But the Avestan *ahura* retained its original good meaning.

Spitama Zarathushtra marked the culminating point of a line of teachers, the *athravans*, who were the fire priests. Zarathushtra's own sermons and teachings are regarded as inspirations from Ahura-Mazda, received as he prayed in front of the sacred fire in the temple.

Dissatisfied with his predecessors' worship of several

ahuras, Zarathushtra dissolved the plurality by his categorical affirmation of the one and only Supreme Being whom he named Ahurao-Mazdao. The name changed in the course of time to Ahura-Mazda, signifying Lord of Life and Wisdom. Single-minded, uncompromising, purely spiritual monotheism – positively opposed to and fiercely intolerant of any deviation from the monotheistic vision – was the quenchless fire that burned in the soul of Zarathushtra.

The Vedic gods to whom warriors prayed for victory – Indra, Saurva (the Indian Shiva), Vayu (in his wicked aspect), Naonhaithya (the two Asvins) – were demonized. Some names of the Vedic *devas*, used in the good sense, became the *yazatas*, or angels, in the Avesta. The outstanding example is Mithra (the Vedic Mitra). Of the others, the Vedic Aryaman is Airyaman, Aramati is Armaiti, Vritraha (Indra as killer of the demon Vritra) is Verethraghna, and Vayu (in his angelic aspect) is Vayu.

Later on, the execrated Soma drink and ceremony came back with an Iranian name, Haoma, and a changed method of preparation. A plant other than the old Soma plant was used together with twigs from the pomegranate tree, and water was poured on them. No fermentation took place and the product was a wholesome non-intoxicating drink.

The main element characterizing the religious split was that those who went southwards through Sogdiana into Bactria became monotheists. Their monotheism touched its peak with Spitama Zarathushtra's conception of Ahura, Lord of Life, conjoined with Mazda, Lord of Wisdom, to make the single Ahura-Mazda, Lord of Life and Wisdom, the One Eternal God, Creator of the universe, God of Righteousness and Truth. From Bactria they spread all over Iran. The religious literature of those Irano-Aryans is the Avesta – most of which was destroyed by Alexander in 331 BC, and still more, a millennium later, by Muslim invaders who shattered the last of the Zarathushtrian Iranian empires (AD 651). Iran then became Muslim.

The other group, as conquering immigrants, went eastwards over the Hindu Kush mountains into the Panjab, the
land of the Indus and its four tributaries. Those Indo-
Aryans took with them the holy book of the erstwhile
undivided Aryans, the Rig-Veda, which has remained a
holy book of the Indo-Aryans and of Hindu India to our
own day. Their religious literature has grown a great deal
through the centuries.

The Rig-Veda contains 1028 hymns, composed by poet-
seers in praise and adoration of several spiritual Beings,
devas, who were 'gods' of Nature's great forces. These gods
were sons of Rita (Eternal Law and Order) and also of Aditi
(the Boundless or Infinite). They were of equal dignity;
there was no superior Overlord. Nevertheless, the Unitary
Wholeness of Transcendence was recognized in the Rig-
Veda (1.164.46) and unequivocally affirmed by the seer
Dirghatamas:

*They call him Indra, Mitra, Varuna, Agni, and he is heavenly
nobly-winged Garutman.*
*To what is one, sages give many a title: they call it Agni, Yama,
Matarisvan.*

We must note carefully that the names of the *devas* are
but titles of the ONE. In practice, theirs was a henotheism.
Each Vedic poet-seer emphasized his own special deity as a
supreme god among others. This was an inclining towards
monotheism. In later centuries the Hindus evolved two
great monotheisms, Vaishnavism and Shaivism.

The Indo-Aryans continued with the worship of the
devas. As the centuries strode past, their saint-sages entered
into the profoundest depths of religious and mystical consciousness in the *turiya* (the fourth) state in meditation.
They experienced in clear consciousness (a transcendent
state in relation to our ordinary consciousness) the answers
to such fundamental questions as 'What is Ultimate Reality?'
and 'Who am I?'. The oldest and greatest Upanishads, like

dazzling, inviolate peaks breathing eternity, live to this day as the monumental evidence of their realization. And there is also that gleaming gem of purest lustre, the Bhagavad Gita, the embodiment of the realization of Unitary Wholeness, which the wise alone can rightly understand, rightly expound, and rightly utilize. And this is true of all pure scriptures and all sensitively intelligent devotees.

The Irano-Aryans also produced their Gita, their Song of Truth, in course of time – The Gathas of Zarathushtra – the first and most important Zarathushtrian scripture composed in the Gathic dialect of the Avestan language. This dialect is more ancient than classical Avestan, just as Vedic preceded classical Sanskrit. The general character of the Avestan dialect, Gathic and classical, agrees almost completely with Vedic, but not so closely with classical Sanskrit which was formed after the separation of the Irano-Aryans and the Indo-Aryans. In fact it is possible to transpose a Gathic verse into Vedic with only slight modifications*.

The Irano-Aryans were immigrants from over the Jaxartes (the Syr Daria) into Eastern Iran, originally inhabited by non-Aryans. Turan (Turkestan), lying on the northern boundary of Eastern Iran, was inhabited by people hostile to the dwellers of Ancient Iran, which stretched from the Tigris to the Indus, from the Araxes (modern Aras) and the Caspian Sea to the Arabian Sea and the Persian Gulf. The Jihun (the Oxus or the Amu Daria) divided the domains of the prehistoric Iranian kings from those of the Turanians. The nomadic Turanians were bitter enemies of the Zarathushtrians, as we gather from the Avesta.

Bactria, the land of Zarathushtra's birth, called Airyanem Vaejah (the land of the Aryans) in the Avesta (Vd.1.3), was ruled by King Vishtaspa. It lay in the north of Eastern Iran. Several of the places mentioned in the Avesta have been identified by scholars: Bakhdi is Balkh (the Bactrian capital);

*I.J.S. Taraporevala in Bulletin of the Deccan College Research Institute, Vol.3. pp.219-224

Sughda is Sogdiana; Mouru is Merv; Haroyu is Herat; Vaekereta is Kabul; Vehrkana is Ancient Hyrcania; Haetumant is the river Helmand; Vouru-kasha (of many bays, world ocean) is the Caspian Sea, the largest sea known to the early Avestan people.

Zarathushtra's date has been a subject of the widest possible difference of opinion between various Greek and Roman writers as well as between modern scholars. Xanthos of Lydia gives about 1800 BC; Aristotle and Eudoxus, 6000 years before Plato; Pliny the Elder (in *Historia Naturalis*, 30.2), several thousand years before Moses, and also 5000 years before the Trojan War; Berosus, 2200 BC. Such dates are unlikely to be correct. Among modern scholars (20th and 19th centuries), Haug, Geiger and R.E. Sanjana suggest the 10th century before Christ, or possibly a little earlier; Herzfeld, about the 5th century BC. In Zarathushtrian literature, in the Bundahesh (Ch. 34), there is a passage which suggests the 7th Century BC – 288 years before Alexander's conquest of Iran in 331 BC. There is strong evidence against this, namely, the closeness of the Gathic dialect to Vedic Sanskrit. Since the date of the Rig-Veda is most probably the 15th century BC, we may reasonably accord between 1400-1200 BC as Zarathustra's date.

Zarathushtra's father, Pourushaspa, came from the family of the Spitamas; his mother, Dughdhova, from the clan of the Hvogvas. Their house was by the banks of the river Dareja* in Airyanem-Vaejah, where also flowed the river Daitya. In this house was Zarathushtra born. He was religiously inclined from his childhood. He firmly believed in one single Supreme Being whom he longed to know personally. Alone, he frequented the banks of the Daitya to pray there and he meditated in seclusion in the mountains. When he was thirty, he had his first vision of Ahura-Mazda. This was followed by six 'conversations' with the Amesha Spentas (the Holy Immortals) and a

*Vd. 19.4: Ys. 9.13.

a 'dialogue' with Ahura-Mazda who imparted the supreme truth to him.

Filled with fervent zeal, he began his missionary work, only to be ridiculed, rejected and obstructed by priests and princes who adhered to the current beliefs and practices of the then prevailing religion in Bactria. Even his own father was not on his side at first. For twelve years he persisted and then decided to win over the Bactrian King Vishtaspa and his consort Queen Hutaosa. He succeeded and also won over a minister of the realm, Frashaoshtra Hvogva, and then his brother Jamaspa Hvogva who was the Prime Minister. The lady Hvovi of the same family married Zarathushtra. The Pahlavi tradition accords to Zarathushtra three sons (Isatvastar, Urvatatnar and Khurshid-Chihar or Hvarchithra) and three daughters (Freni, Thriti, Pouruchista).

Thereafter his mission as Prophet and Reformer spread far and wide over all Iran and met with complete success*. It is recorded[†] that Zarathushtrian missionaries spread the gospel as far as India and China.

Tradition has it that when Zarathushtra was 77 years old, King Vishtaspa went to Seistan as the guest of Zal, the warrior who was the father of the great hero Rustam. Vishtaspa's father, Lohrasp, King of Iran, was praying together with Zarathushtra in the Atash Behram (the fire temple) of Balkh. It happened that there was no military leader at this juncture to protect the country. Its hereditary enemy, King Arjasp of Turan, seized the opportunity to attack. Old King Lohrasp was slain in the temple. So too was Zarathushtra, by the javelin of the Turanian Bratvarxsh, also known as Turbaratur.

Of the founders of the great religions, Moses (aged 120) died a natural death, the Buddha (aged 80) and Muhammed

---

*Vahishta-Ishti Gatha, Ys.53.1.
[†]A.V.W. Jackson, Zoroaster, The Prophet of Ancient Iran, New York, 1899. (pp.278-280.)

(aged 62) died after falling ill; Krishna, Jesus and some of
the Sikh Gurus suffered violent deaths. We have considerable information about the lives of the Buddha, Muhammed
and the Sikh Teachers; less about Moses and Jesus;
extremely little about Zarathushtra.

The millennia following the death of each of the founders of
the established religions of the world have seen the
emergence of mystics, philosophers of religion, and poets
and artists of genius who have developed or expanded the
teachings of the founders. The Christian, Muslim, Hindu
and Jewish worlds have a galaxy of them. In the Buddhist
world the vision and expositions of such men gave birth to
Mahayana and Zen which are markedly innovative.

But there has also been degeneration in each case, leading to the sprouting of various sects, superstitions and
absurd ideas. Whereas the founders, Perfected Holy Ones,
made affirmations of the living Truth shining with the light
of Transcendence – affirmations which were of a unique
nature, outstandingly original, unconstrained by the limitations of the cultural conditioning of their race, times and
prevailing circumstances – their well-meaning devotees
and followers, however intellectual and pure-living, had
not that freedom of the Spirit and that incomparable lustre
of insight into divine Truth that their Teachers possessed.
Usually they were humble souls, disciplined, loyal and
self-effacing. What light they could shed was attributed to
the Master's inspiration and grace. Hence, their insights
tended to be presented as words spoken by their long dead
Teachers. We find this in the later Avestan and the later
Buddhist texts, to give but two examples: 'Zarathushtra
said . . .' or 'The Lord said . . .' Did they actually say so in
their lifetime in all cases? Truth is more important than
enthusiasm, however fervent or devoted.

So, while the immediate, spiritual Children of the Master
– who were the promise of the New Dawn – did produce

ambrosia for mortals hungering for God's Truth, their successors through the centuries lost their angelic wings and lumbered along loading their fold with ponderous commentaries, questionable exegeses, and dull, unfruitful polemics and apologetics. (Neither Truth nor Transcendence needs any defence). Time and again they brought division not unity, confusion not clarity, discord not peace, darkness not light, gloom not bliss into the lives of the people whom they imagined they were serving and salving. (Though it should be added there have been exceptions, by God's Grace – lone lights in a vast celestial desert.)

After Zarathushtra's death, a slow decline set in. The movement from the Gathas to the later Avesta was retrograde. There was an increasing tendency towards complexity and concreteness. In the Gathas, the Amesha-Spentas (though not yet specifically designated by that term) represented cardinal virtues functioning transcendentally on a divine plane, the plane of Ahura-Mazda Himself; in the later Avesta the texts are concerned with their healing powers, with formulae for magical spells to drive away the demons of death and disease. Furthermore, several of the *devas* of the old Indo-Iranian days, expelled by Zarathushtra, returned one by one; the refugee gods found Zarathushtrian homes. During the Pahlavi period (the 3rd to the 9th century AD), the decline reached its nadir.

The founders personally realized the state of Revelation, the one-ness in Transcendence, as actuality and not merely as pious belief or anxious hope. They affirmed that realization unequivocally in simple terms. The Upanishadic Teachers declared *aham brahma'smi* – 'I am Brahman'. Shri Krishna, the Lord incarnate, revealed to Arjuna: 'I am the Father of this universe, the Mother, the Supporter, the Origin of the Father, the Holy One to be known, the Creative Word' (B.G.,9.18) and 'I am the Atman seated in the heart of all beings' (B.G.,10.20). Jesus affirmed: 'I and my

Father are one' (John, 10.30), and he admitted to Caiaphas,
the high priest who questioned him, that he was the son of
God (Mark, 14.61,62). al-Hallaj said *ana'l haqq*, 'I am the
Creative Word,' for which the Muslims crucified him cruel-
ly. The Buddha affirmed in no uncertain terms that he was
the supremely self-enlightened Perfected One. Muhammed
made no claim to union with God. He insisted that the
Quran, the scripture given to him, was a final restatement
of the faith delivered to the Prophets before him – Abraham,
Moses, Jesus – confirming their scriptures, the Quran itself
being confirmed by them, and that he was simply the
Apostle of Allah. What Zarathushtra said of himself will be
considered in the following chapters.

It may be asked what evidence is there that these affirmations of union in Transcendence or God are wholly true?
Are they the fantasies of disordered minds? Or wicked lies
by conscience-less exploiters? Or knavish tricks by self-
centred megalomaniacs serving their own evil power-lust?

We may know them, first by their holy lives, spent entirely in the service of God and man. Second by the fact that
their personal example and teachings have comforted and
inspired countless followers to live the good life*; that the
teachings have spread far beyond the boundaries of their
own country and society and have definitely affected history for better and also for worse (the latter due to the flaws
in the character and intelligence of the followers). Third, by
the fact that if one lives in accord with their teachings it is
possible to realize what they realized, though it is admit-
tedly a task fraught with very great difficulty. And fourth,
by the astonishing spiritual energy and vitality which has
enabled the teachings to survive for long ages.

In connection with the previous paragraph, we must be
well aware that it is essential to ask the right question(s),
and make sure that we are well qualified to give full and just

*Although the human race has not made a particularly creditable showing in this
respect.

consideration to the answer(s) received or to the evidence obtained in the course of an unbiassed and unprejudiced investigation.

The realization of Transcendence involves a transmutation of one's mode of awareness of the Total Reality. One's consciousness can function not only in the ordinary mode in our worldly context but also in a transcendent mode in a transcendent context which subsumes the worldly context. This is by far the most important element in the lives of all the truly realized spiritual Teachers (including of course the founders of the great religions). This we must keep well in mind in our considerations of Zarathushtra and his teachings in the following chapters.

2

The Nature of the Transmutation of Zarathushtra's Consciousness

Whoso through his purification, enlightenment and compassion has become the true and perfect human is thereafter the instrument of Transcendence. From him there flows the teaching which spells salvation for all beings. His whole life, in thought and feeling, speech and action, is a source of inspiration for all to live the Good Life, the Holy Life.

Such a being was Zarathushtra the Prophet of Ancient Iran.

He declared:

When I beheld Thee in my very eyes, then I realized Thee in my mind, O Mazda, as the First and also the Last of all eternity, as the Father of Vohu Manah, as the true Creator of Asha, as Lord of all actions of man. (Ys.31.8)

Now in truth I have beheld Him clearly in my mind's eye. Knowing through Asha of the Good Spirit in word and deed, I can now see Mazda Ahura Himself. (Ys.45.8)

At the time when Thou didst command me, 'Go to Asha in fulness of knowledge' Thou hadst not revealed to me things unheard of; but Thou didst reveal them when, to dispel all darkness before me, Sraosha, Divine Obedience, accompanied by the blessing of Divine Light, arose within me. (Ys.43.12)

Then did I realise Thee as the Most Bountiful One, O Mazda Ahura, when the Good Mind encircled me completely. He declared to me that silent meditation is the best for attaining spiritual enlightenment. (Ys.43.15)

When the full power of the Good Mind came upon me, then did I realize Thee as the Mighty and Most Bountiful One, O Mazda, for I saw that the same hand with which Thou dost promote men's destinies, Thou also assignest their just dues to the followers of the Druj (the Evil One) and to the followers of Asha through the energy of The Flaming Fire all-powerful through Thy law. (Ys.43.4)

Then did I realize Thee as the Most Bountiful One, O Mazda Ahura, when I beheld Thee as the First at the birth of life. Since Thou didst ordain that deeds and words shall bear fruit, evil comes to the evil, and good blessings to the good. Thy wisdom ordains it so till the final consummation of creation. (Ys.43.5)

Then did I realize Thee as the Most Bountiful One when the Good Mind encircled me completely. When I first became enlightened through Thy Words, Thou didst teach me how hard it is to induce faith among mankind, yet will I practise what Thou declarest to me is the best. (Ys.43.11.)

What do these affirmations mean? What is their significance? What are their implications? What kind of a being was Zarathushtra?

Suppose you and I studied philosophy and attained an equal standard at University. If so, we are likely to have understood each other fairly well when engaged in a philosophical discussion. But if, as the years passed, you proved to be a genius whose perceptions penetrated far more deeply than mine, I would find it very difficult, perhaps impossible, to keep pace with your insights or to understand you at all. The vision with which you will have become familiar and the sphere in which your consciousness functions as easily as if on home ground will be like 'a world beyond' to me. Why? Not merely because your thought has gone far ahead of mine (for one can 'catch up' with another's thought), not only because your intellectual perceptivity is keener than mine (for that can be developed by one or another type of mental training) but essentially because your consciousness has evolved to a state more intensely sensitive and enlightened than mine. In other words, your *mode of awareness of reality has undergone a transformation.*

Through the operation of our senses in our ordinary worldly state, all of us are conscious of every object, circumstance and event as separate from us, and of our own self as a particular entity exclusive of all other selves and creatures. We are separatively and isolatively self-conscious. Our psycho-physical organism is the self, of which we are vividly conscious; whereas each particular object or person or the universe as a whole, is the not-self, the *other* thing or creature or world, of which we are only relatively conscious most of the time.

In our ordinary worldly state, we see the entire universe as a *collection* of separate objects, creatures, events, etc. Each and every one of these is finite, and therefore quantitatively measurable and qualitatively characterizable; it is dynamic and temporal, undergoing constant change, and therefore, when the final change takes place, it is mortal. For us as we are, our universal context is a context of the finite, temporal and mortal. Our usual mode of awareness is the mode of finitude, temporality and mortality.

Hence we are not clearly conscious of the close relationships between everything constituting the universe. In actual fact, as modern science has shown us, the universe is a *living whole,* just as each one of us is a living whole organically and spiritually. Some of us may feel or believe this is so and hold it firmly as a reasonable idea or an intellectual conviction. But believing, or thinking, or being convinced is not the same as being fully and clearly conscious. If and when we are fully and clearly conscious, *that* non-separative, enlightened consciousness is Creative Energy which is pure Action, natural and spontaneous, quite often no longer involving a conceptual-verbal knowing by the brain. It is, so to say, an 'unknowing knowing' – a knowing by 'being' which is a 'doing'. It transcends the consciousness which functions in our incompletely evolved state.

Consider, for instance, a child just born. The limbs of this neonate can only make spasmodic movements, undeliberate and not known ('known' in our ordinary meaning of the word) by his brain. As he grows, he goes through the stages of crawling, standing and toddling, maintaining his balance with a little help. He is now becoming conscious of his limbs and body, and 'knows what to do'. He next walks more freely, lifting his legs over an obstacle or pushing it aside. Then the urge and excitement for speedier movement comes into play. He runs. His brain knowledge of how to run, avoid obstacles etc. grows. Later still, he runs freely, conscious of himself as the knowing subject running over the ground towards a desired goal as the object. Discriminative consciousness and the analytical brain are still functioning here – he has to think about it as he is doing it.

Finally there comes the climactic point, as the perfect runner is realized. He runs with such perfection that we say he does it *un*consciously – it all just happens, naturally. But what we call 'doing it *un*consciously' is precisely Action which is Pure Consciousness in perfect manifestation physically. The *free* Action happens in *perfection*.

Again, watch and listen to an accomplished pianist. He is one with his instrument as he plays with carefree naturalness. We say, 'He plays so effortlessly.' But consider the stages he went through. First the considerable effort of technical training and memorizing; next, the concentrated activity of the brain, listening critically to the quality of the tones he is producing, expressively evoking the wordless message of the music. Finally there is the pianist's consciousness culminating as physical Action embodying transcendent Beauty.

The evolution of consciousness culminates in the transformation of our ordinary mode of awareness – in terms of finitude, temporality and mortality – into a transcendent mode. The context of this mode is infinity, eternity and immortality, which is also the context of Religion, of perfect religious living, of Transcendence itself. We must not make the all too common mistake of thinking this is another world, something impossible for us ordinary mortals even to conceive, leave alone to aspire to and live up to. Transcendence completely subsumes our limited context of finitude and mortality; it does not annihilate it. That is, not only does the unitary infinity, eternity and immortality completely *contain* the multitudinous finite, temporal and mortal but also altogether *interpenetrates* it in the most wonderful way. The whole of infinity, all of eternity, is *totally embodied in every single particular*, from an atom to a galaxy, from a virus to a perfected saint, throughout the entire universe. Thus we can understand that verily there is One Total Reality; and that it is shortsighted to talk and think in terms of 'this' world and 'that' world.

Since the One Total Reality is of this nature, there is intimate relationship between the finite and infinite, the temporal and the eternal, the mortal and the immortal. All this was of supreme concern to Zarathushtra and to all the Perfected Holy Ones.

Zarathushtra and founders of the great religions, and all true spiritual teachers, having realized Transcendence, were able to be aware in the mode of infinity and eternity. Their clear consciousness could function freely in that transcendent mode as and when they entered and abided in it of their own accord or whenever Transcendence, manifesting grace, bestowed it upon them. Equally, they could also function in the usual finite and temporal mode of us ordinary mortals, with at least one outstanding difference, namely that, whereas we are so liable to delusion and illusion, misunderstanding and misinterpretation with respect to the psyche, they were free of all that when functioning in this finite mortal sphere by virtue of the perfect purity of their psyche and the clear-sightedness of their intellect.

And yet, even the holiest, enlightened ones could not escape all the limitations imposed upon them by the inadequacy of language, of everyday conceptualizing and verbalizing, when they tried to communicate the truth of the transcendent context to those in the finite, mortal context.

In fact that Truth can never be communicated by any one to any other who is not capable of being completely silent in body and mind. If you, the Holy One, are present, and if I can stay completely silent, free of any conceptualizing and verbalizing, fully sensitive, all sense functions pacified (pacified, not anaesthetized and ceasing to function), then the transcendent state can supervene and the Truth will be realized by the silent mind. There will be a transformation of the mode of awareness out of the finite state into the Immeasurable.

This can also happen without the presence of the human who has flowered as the Perfected Holy One, for Transcendence itself, the Absolute Holy, is omnipresent. The Infinite Eternal 'speaks' with the tongue of Revelation, whereas I speak with my awkward and inefficient tool of concept and word. Revelation's 'speech' is simply a single tone, the Creative Vibration of the Infinite Eternal, whose Immortality negates my small sphere of mortality, without destroying it, even though – wondrous Grace! – it brings imperfect subhuman me and all mortality into being by voluntary self-constriction into material manifestation, its own crucifixion. Even though it negates – without eliminating – all mortality, it nevertheless permeates it wholly and, with infinite patience, awaits its transmutation, and – wondrous Mercy! – restores it into its own Infinite Eternal Immortality.

Is all this mere verbiage? In a sense it is! But, if by any chance it sparks you into the light of Transcendence, you too will produce your verbiage, hopefully a little less inadequate through progress than mine. If and when someone's words have this effect upon you, then those words are prophetic speech. Thus will it go on until a purified humanity has so evolved that it can dispense with the concept and word, and mind will converse with mind without intermediary.

Layman and scholar alike mistakenly speak of the 'thought' of the Perfected Holy Ones. The thinking of the Holy Ones is not like the 'thinking' of us ordinary mortals – which is mainly a stream of inaudible talk, concepts and words expressing our dim-lit consciousness not yet evolved to the full fruition possible to the human. The transcendent Awareness of the Perfected Holy One is an enlightened Consciousness. Its MIND-ING is direct seeing, *unerring* insight – a timeless conjugation with Truth – in fact, a-having-become-the-Truth. The Holy One is the living Light of Revelation, for through him as the psycho-physical exis-tent, the Transcendent Consciousness constantly radiates Truth, Life and Healing. Thought is no container for Revelation. Thought often falsifies and pollutes Revelation although, exceptionally, it might move some of its light-obscuring thunderclouds close enough to produce lightning flashes out of Transcendence. But even a single transcen-dent flash of Revelation can wipe clean much of the thinking, conceptualizing and philosophizing by the imperfect mortal trying to represent Transcendence by means of the tools of the finite and temporal, viz. that which has emerged out of energy-mass, space-time, motion and matter – the realm ruled by Death.

Once this transmutative event has taken place, the gui-dance by the Wisdom-gone-beyond enables the Holy One to witness the pacification and subsidence of the turmoil of thinking into tranquil quiescence. And then the Peace which passes all understanding supervenes, and prevails throughout his life. Furthermore, he sees clearly that the proper function and place of thought and concept lies in the sphere of dealing with matter in our bodily life, and of developing and applying the skills required for earning one's living, manipulating machines, crossing the road and dealing with all the problems that characterize our everyday world. Thought and concept play a major role in acquiring all our worldly knowledge – arts, science, mathematics, industry, engineering, cooking, dressing, gardening, medicine, surgery, teaching etc.; and also in the use of our senses and in decision-making in the practical, worldly life.

But thought and concept are the accumulation and result of past experience through the ages, stored in mankind's memory. They tend to hold us back, preventing progressive emergence into the new. Up to a point, the heritage of the past conserves and nurtures and keeps life going in terms of preserving the status quo – which makes for the opportunity, and allows us time, for right circumspection. But if we cling to the forms of our traditional heritage long after it has passed its fruitive point, and grimly hold on to outworn fixations, we decay and fossilize.

The founders of the great religions and all the true spiritual teachers of the world saw all this with faultless clarity. They saw that it was their destiny to help those mortals who cared for Truth to realize human fruition and fulfil the purpose of their existence. These aspirants were but few – the majority neither cared nor were genuinely interested. Yet the Holy Ones always gave themselves wholly for the sake of even one person's welfare, for they knew that the whole universe is at work in producing and nurturing each individual, and that each individual's salvation promotes the world's well-being.

Earlier (p.18), it was mentioned that the Holy One, in whom the evolution of consciousness had reached its culmination, could be aware in the Transcendent as well as in the worldy mode. He was 'at home' in either, or simultaneously in both contexts – namely the Infinite Eternal, and the finite mortal. It was also said that these two contexts were One Total Reality in actuality. I, the finite mortal, *talk*

and think in terms of two contexts because my consciousness, not yet fully evolved, is compulsorily confined to
functioning in terms of duality and multiplicity. I am conscious isolatively and separatively, not holistically or
unitarily. Only in certain situations is this not so. For
instance, whilst the psycho-physical organism is perfectly
healthy, I am aware of it as a 'one-thing'. When I have an
ache or a disease in some constituent organ, I am aware of a
separate part, and I disssociate the 'I' from that part. I want
to be free of the pain or disease, to be rid of it. Note well: I
don't want to be rid of the organ or any part of the organism;
but I do want it to be healed, so that there is a restoration to
the state of the 'one-thing' wholeness, the state of holiness.

Again, consider just one outstanding contrast between
our two contexts. The finite and temporal, of which I am at
present actually conscious, is measurable and describable,
whereas the Infinite Eternal, which all of us can postulate,
is immeasurable and is non-descript (although maybe we
can say a few suggestive words about it). The Infinite
Eternal is not experienced by us through any of our senses;
and we are unable to be actually conscious of it as vividly as
we are conscious of objects, persons and all that we ordinarily experience. Limitation characterizes our objective
world. So it is measurable. We can use instruments to help
us to measure that which is not directly perceivable by the
senses; but even here, the final step is to *see* only pointer
readings or impressions on a photographic plate, etc.

Although we are familiar with space, we have no means
for measuring it as a particular entity. If, and only if, we
limit it by, say, a structure consisting of four enclosing
walls, a floor and a roof, can we measure the volume of
space contained within that limiting structure. The actual
measurements made are the distances between floor and
roof and the two pairs of opposing walls, all of which are
solid material *in* space. By imposing all these necessary
limitations, and then by imposing the mental limitations of

our arbitrary measures of length, breadth and depth and of our definition of volume as the product of these three measures, can we state that the volume of that confined space is so much. Note that we do not talk of a 'length (or a breadth) *of* space'; we only say a 'distance of so many (man-conceived) units', the distance being determined by two fixed points or objects *in* space. Space itself we cannot measure in the manner in which we measure a piece of cloth.

So, too, with time. We have to set up arbitrary limiting measures of duration with various instruments, material or electrical or atomic, impose our arbitrary standards of measurement and thus obtain a measure of what we call time (as duration). But *time itself* – the rhythm or context of the living process of all things, or organisms, or the whole cosmos – we cannot measure.

If we cannot measure the space or time of which we are conscious as our context, how much more so must immeasurability characterize the context of Infinity (the *non*-finite) and of Eternity (the *non*-temporal).

The nature of Consciousness of the Immeasurable is unimaginable and inconceivable. Imagination and conception are confined to the realm of finitude and temporality (and therefore of mortality). Almost all the world defines Infinity as the opposite of finitude, and thus it is made into an 'other' to the finite; and Eternity as the opposite of time, an 'other' to temporality. But this means that consciousness is not functioning in terms of unitary wholeness. It is being forced to function in terms of duality. Furthermore, Eternity is regarded as synonymous with timelessness. This is not so, for timelessness prevails during a limited human experience, which is bounded by specific points in time marking its beginning and ending. The experience itself is not the full Consciousness of Eternity but of a period of obliviousness to, or of unawareness of the passage of time. Obliviousness occurs when one suffers from intoxication, or is anaesthetized, or has lost consciousness. Unawareness occurs when one enters, or is granted, the *Unio Mystica*, which is only a foreshadowing of Eternity, blissful peace though it be.

Thus we are almost always conscious in the mode of duality at least, often of multiplicity. Consciousness in the mode of unitary wholeness is the spiritual freedom for man towards which he is evolving. This mode of awareness does not wipe out consciousness as it functions now; it wholly subsumes it, intensifies it and clarifies it. Thereby, various dormant faculties of Mind are released into active functioning.

Zarathushtra realized (made real) the state of the Perfected Holy One.

Such a being, longing to help his fellow human beings to realize for themselves the Holy State and serve the unfolding purposes and activity of Transcendence, is always confronted with a very difficult problem. How is He, when His mode of Awareness is Transcendent, functioning in the context of Infinity and Eternity, to present what is realized in that Transcendent mode – to beings who are confined to the realm of concepts and words, whose psyches are tainted with so many defilements, who are the slaves of their pleasure drive and ambition, self-orientedness and self-seeking, their lusts and greeds, hates and violence, their anxieties and fears, attachments and aversions, their illusions and delusions, their ignorance and stupidity, and who do not genuinely care for Truth and Purity, Wisdom and Love, for Peace and Harmony?

Furthermore, what kind of language can he use to speak of the Transcendent Holy to the people? All the words of all the languages of the world denote and connote all that belongs to the worldly consciousness, to the context of the finite and mortal, the realm ruled by Death. There are very few exceptions to this, and most of them simply negate the finite and mortal – words like in-finity, im-mortality, un-imaginable, in-conceivable, in-destructible, birth-less,

death-less, beginning-less, end-less, measure-less, etc. –
only *suggesting* the context of Life Eternal. All words and
thoughts have meaning for us ordinary mortals only within
duality or multiplicity. Only within the confines of duality
do we converse, when using audible speech or the written
word of any known language as our means of communica-
tion. There are no words in any language which the Holy
Ones can use for making positive statements regarding the
Infinite Eternal. All expression by us is limited. It belongs
to the sphere of mortality. Transcendence, the unitary
whole, is beyond all expression. It is the inexpressible
Absolute. The multi-dimensional cannot be packed into a
point. Nonetheless, precisely this *is* the Mystery, the
Miracle. What we cannot do, the Absolute can – for it
expresses (presses out of itself) the entire cosmos. And in
every single one of these countless manifestations composing the universe is embodied the whole of Transcendence.
(It is easier to understand this if we divest the word 'whole'
of size and quantity).

So all the Holy Ones became living exemplars, as well as
expounders, of *the way man should live his daily life* in order
that the complete purification of his whole being could take
place. In the process of such purification, the transformation
of his mode of awareness goes on, his consciousness evolves
towards its full fruition, culminating in the Transcendent
awakening to the Infinite Eternal. No words and concepts
are thereafter needed by him.

Zarathushtra understood this for himself. But, in order
to communicate with others, he *had* to use the language
spoken by his own people. The Holy Ones do not build up
a thesis; they make positive Affirmations, aphorismic,
epigrammatic, in the language of their time.

It is very significant that these Affirmations deeply affect
those who are sensitive and receptive – and influence their
whole life for good.

3
Exposition of some Teachings

Let us now consider some of Zarathushtra's Affirmations quoted in the previous chapter. From these, as from several others, we gather that Zarathushtra and Ahura Mazda 'speak' with each other. The divine dialogue is a distinguishing feature in monotheistic religions. Man asks questions. God answers. Man prays for guidance. God instructs. But God is not a creature, not even a supernatural creature or a superhuman man with a mouth that speaks human languages. God is spoken of by people as the Supreme Being, the Transcendent Creator of every creature and every thing; as the Immortal, the Eternal, the Infinite, the Living; as All-wise, Almighty, Omniscient, Omnipresent; as the all-Compassionate, all-Merciful, Forgiving, Bountiful; Perfect Justiciar, Healer, etc.

Consider all these terms carefully. Most of them apply, though only in minor degree, to man, who maximises them and applies them to God. Thus the God projected out of man's imaginings is no other than man apotheosized, an idol. This is not to deny the reality – the Transcendent Reality – of God. The anthropomorphic God is perhaps a picture of what man himself would like to be and sometimes aspires to be. God is beyond man as he is at present, altogether beyond. Man the procreator is a faint shadow of God the Creator. Man may be the measure of all things, but God is the Immeasurable Transcendent invisibly embodied in everything, the subtle and hidden divine potential in all creatures and all things. Man has to wake up to this. To us ordinary mortals, God as God is the Unknown and Unknowable, for no knowing whilst consciousness functions in our finite mortal state can ever penetrate into the context of the Infinite Eternal.

In the Ahuramazda Yasht of the later Avesta, Zarathushtra asks Ahura Mazda (God) to reveal his Names which are the *holiest, mightiest, fairest, most effective for overcoming evil, and which are best for Healing.* (Ahuramazda Yasht, para 11)

Ahura Mazda gives a long list of Names (paras. 13-21), in which are included most of the terms mentioned at the beginning of this chapter.

He proceeds (para. 33) to make a most significant statement:

O, Zarathushtra, here in my abode dwelleth Vohu-Manah, Asha-Vahishta, Khshathra Vairya, Spenta Armaiti, Haurvatat and Ameretat.

These six Names respectively mean the Good (Perfect) Mind, Righteousness (Virtue, the Divine Law, Purity), Power (Creative Energy), Holy Devotion (Adoring, Worshipping Heart), Wholeness (Holiness, Health), and Immortality. In the later Avesta, after Zarathushtra's death, they are called Amesha Spentas, the Holy Immortals. They are regarded as individual Celestial Beings (like Archangels) by many Zarathushtrians; others regard these Names as representative of the outstandingly distinctive characteristics or powers of Ahura Mazda.

'Here in my abode' says Ahura Mazda. What is this 'abode'? This abode is Ahura Mazda's own constitution, the very being of God. Here in Transcendence, What and Who, Substance and Spirit are identical, Unitarily Whole, the Holy Alone. Space cannot confine Transcendence nor can time limit it. Ahura Mazda is neither personal nor impersonal. Transpersonal, unrestricted to im-personality, Ahura Mazda, Lord of Life and Wisdom, is Ahura Mazda, beyond all names, all characteristics, all space and time. Transcending all being and non-being, Ahura Mazda is the Infinite-Eternal, and the Infinite-Eternal is Ahura Mazda.

We sub-human* mortals, because of our spiritual impotence, our intellectual shortcomings, our over-weening self-conceit and our fear-ridden psyche, have through the ages presented Transcendence as an idol, a dumb graven image of clay or wood or metal, or as an entity, a super-human Person or Being. But any and every manifested entity is finite and mortal, for it has a beginning (birth) a proceeding (a temporal life-span) and an ending (death). Is it any wonder that all the man-made gods have found their graves in limbo?

All this has happened because we have been, and still are, conscious only in terms of of finitude, temporality and mortality.

Nevertheless, as stated earlier, during the last six thousand years or so there have arisen, one here, one there, those in whom consciousness evolved to the full flowering possible to man. They, the Holy Ones, awoke, clearly and fully enlightened, to the Infinite-Eternal, the Unitary Whole, the One Total Reality, the Truth.

When the Perfected Holy One is in that fully-awakened and actively-functioning Consciousness, he is no longer separate from the Absolute. He is in perfect communion with his Lord. His whole psycho-physical organism undergoes a transformation and the brain becomes so sensitive and acute that concepts and words – suggestive, inspiring, not inadequate, not misleading – may emerge. The speech of the Holy One is then prophetic speech.

Zarathushtra himself, in that profoundest Consciousness of the Unitary Whole, *is* Ahura Mazda. Zarathushtra in his ordinary state as the psycho-physical person, communicating the nature of Ahura Mazda to his fellow humans in his land, uses the names of the Amesha Spentas to suggest the Reality of Ahura Mazda, to indicate that which constitutes

---

*This term is not being used in a pejorative sense. It means those members of the human species who have not yet reached the culmination of human evolution. We are still part beast, part human – a sub-stage of full humanity.

Ahura Mazda. So it is not as if Ahura Mazda *has* Vohu Manah, Asha, Khshathra, Armaiti, Haurvatat and Ameretat, but actually *is* Divine Intelligence (the Good Mind), the divine Law and Order (Righteousness, Virtue), Power (the primordial Creative Energy), Divine Devotion (Transcendent Love), Wholeness (Holiness) and Immortality (deathlessness, Eternity).

Since the context of Transcendence is the Infinite Eternal, the whole of Ahura Mazda is the whole of divine Intelligence, the whole of Creative Energy, etc. There is no possibility of fragmentation or fragmentariness for the Unitary Whole in the context of the Infinite-Eternal. Only by deliberate self-constriction, the One becomes the countless many.

How may we, ordinary mortals, try to understand Ahura Mazda? Begin with Khshathra, the primordial undifferentiated Creative Energy. In its own transcendent context, it is eternally active in a state of vibrant (living) quiescence. Armaiti's influence of Transcendent Love gives rise to a stir in Transcendence. Khshathra, Creative Energy, and Vohu Manah, Absolute Consciousness (or Pure Mind), release grades of manifestation in a descending sequence of differentiated forms in which Consciousness becomes increasingly unaware of its original free state, and Energy becomes increasingly concretized till it reaches its grossest form as matter. Vohu Manah is that archetypal expression of the primordial undifferentiated Creative Energy which is the formative Power which infuses Asha, constitutively, into every single differentiated particular in each and every grade. Thus the Cosmos has its inherent Law and Order.

Ahura Mazda, essentially as Asha, embodied in every person and in everything, is the supreme means for the perfect fulfilment of everything and every man, and for the liberation of the self-constricted Ahura Mazda into the absolute freedom of Ahura Mazda's original unrestricted Unitary Wholeness.

The wise devotee might now sense the purpose of his existence and the Way to its fulfilment.

Throughout the millennia man has anthropomorphized his understanding or vision of the Creative Source and controlling power of the universe. The gods and godlings of all the pantheons of all human cultures are super-humans; time and again they are not so super in their personal inter-relationships; sometimes they 'enjoy sweet dalliance' with mortals and generate semi-divine heroes, man-gods, or, as in India, saintly sages. The point to note here is that man, when projecting his god-conceptions out of his brain, cannot avoid the consequences of the limitations imposed upon his inner consciousness. Man is thus and thus in his nature and behaviour, and similarly his gods are also thus and thus, except that they are so on the grand scale. His statement that the gods are immortal is true in a limited way. The powers, qualities, skills, abilities and behaviour attributed to the gods and goddesses represent in maximum degree the powers and attributes of ordinary mortals. As long as mankind in its sub-human state in which consciousness has not reached the peak point of its evolution, exists, its gods will continue to exist, displaying their godliness and ungodliness in their way just as we display our humanity and sub-humanity – and all too often our inhumanity – in our way. When mankind will have truly realized its Humanity, and consciousness will have flowered in Action which is ever Pure and Beautiful, Free and Creative, then no more gods will be projected out of men's brains. That will take a very long time.

Meanwhile, there is a danger that man, like a lunatic criminal, might exterminate himself before long. But if sub-human man succeeds in remaining free of this danger, learns to live sensibly and realizes true Humanity during the full span of his existence on this planet, then that span will be the measure of the actual temporal existence of his brain-projected gods. For then Perfected Holy Ones will walk the Earth. And such Persons, true Humans, will not project any gods.

The Perfected Holy One becomes, in mind and innermost consciousness, his realized Vision. Note carefully: he not merely sees or understands with his brain etc., but actually *becomes* the Vision, the Truth etc. The chrysalis becomes the butterfly, the bud becomes the flower. This implies the non-existence – the 'death' – of the chrysalis or bud, the death which is not destruction or annihilation but a transformation or transmutation into the New – a progressive emergence into the New. Likewise, sub-human man dies to all evil in him, outgrows his imperfections, and emerges as the full-fledged true Human, thus fulfilling one purpose of his existence.

Zarathushtra flowers as a Perfected Holy One. His psyche is utterly pure, empty of all obstructions to the Light of Transcendence, no longer suffering from ambivalence. His Mind is one with the Divine Mind (Vohu-Manah). His consciousness functions not only in the mortal context of the finite and temporal but can also enter and abide in the transcendent context of the Infinite Eternal. And the Names of the Amesha Spentas express the nature of this transcendent realization in innermost consciousness – a distinguishing mark of all Perfected Holy Ones.

In Transcendence, the Ultimate Unity is the real Fact. Comparison has no place here. There can be comparison only in the context of duality. When there is true Wholeness (*Haurvatat*), each particular is perfect, incomparable. If your body is absolutely healthy, how can you compare the efficiency of your heart with that of your liver? Or any one perfect cell with any other perfect cell?

If only mankind had understood this and lived by it, man's history would never have been stained by the wars and cruelties perpetrated in the name of religion. That such things have happened, and are still happening, is evidence of man's desecration of Religion.

When the Holy One's Consciousness is active in the
transcendent context, he is in the *Unio Mystica*, one in
Transcendence. It is incorrect to say he has *attained* Transcendence or *achieved* union with God. What has happened
is that by virtue of perfect purity (the absence of every
vestige of selfness), his whole being – mind and consciousness and the psycho-physical organism – is entirely open to
Transcendence. It is Transcendence which fulfils itself as
the Perfect Human through that man, and thereby proves
its transcendence as the Supreme.

Each time the *Unio Mystica* takes place, it leaves an inera-
dicable impress on the psycho-physical organism. This
impress may sometimes give rise to a conceptual and verbal
formulation after the Holy One comes out of the transcendent state and consciousness functions again in the limited
context of the finite and mortal. Such formulations constitute the religious and spiritual teachings of the Holy Ones.

This formulation at the psycho-physical level of the
impress made by the psycho-spiritual Union with Transcendence is the meaning of God and the Holy One speaking
with each other. God graciously grants the ineffable Revelation by pure, stainless, spiritual conjugation. The Holy
One speaks with awe-inspired reverence and deep humility.

*With uplifted hands and deep humility, I beseech, O Mazda,
first and foremost this, the abiding joy of Thy Holy Spirit.*
(Ys.28.1)

*O Mazda, He who through Asha, and with humility, spreads
abroad in his speech the Holy Word is a friend to Zarathushtra.*
(Ys.50.6)

*The industrious individual, just in action, full of godly wisdom
in humility, who is dedicated to the upright prophet becomes
the blessed ruler of the world through his Perceptive Wisdom.*
(Ys.51.5)

*In humility we bow before you, O Honoured Powers, seeking
the Joy of Mazda.* (Ys.51.20)

God's Revelation is of the Infinite Eternal, the Immortal. The Holy One's speech, however profound or inspiring, sublime or simple, has perforce lost a few or several dimensions of Divinity in the constricting descent out of the Infinite into the finite. Yet it is charged with such transcendent Power and Truth and Beauty that it outlasts the decrepitude and decay of all the products of frail mortality through a hundred generations, and remains as fragrant throughout its age-long blossoming as in its primal emergence. How marvellous is divine Transcendence!

God (or Transcendence) is not an Other, separate from me – however lowly or sub-human or even bestial I may be. My confinement to the sub-human state means that my consciousness has not yet awakened to Godhood – not 'my' Godhood which is merely my imperfect (sometimes misshapen and harmful) God-conception projected out of my brain, but to Godhood the Transcendent Real, the Infinite Eternal. God completely subsumes me. It is my ignorance of this supreme spiritual Truth which prevents the light of Transcendence enveloping me. When I am fully awake, the sense of a separate 'me' – due to the isolative self-consciousness of the subject – completely vanishes, and there is only God, Transcendence Alone. This total vanishing of 'me', the isolated subject, the 'I', is the absolute fulfilment of God, and of 'me'.

This vanishing of 'me' does not mean that the living psycho-physical person referred to by the word 'I' has perished. It means that this person's ordinary self-awareness in isolative terms, because of which he is conscious of himself as the observing subject separate from and thus not fully related to the universe, has undergone a complete transformation. No longer is it a case of 'I-am-I and not you' or 'My self is not the not-self' but a *vivid, real, constant consciousness* (not a mere idea or belief) that 'I *am* you, and you *are* me; you and I are but varying forms of each other, the variation simply contributing to the richness of us two as a single whole. My self *is* the not-self and the world *is* me, wholly, completely.' The consciousness of the unbroken wholeness of the Totality is so intense that the *isolativeness and separativeness* of ordinary self-consciousness has utterly vanished. Self-consciousness is indispensable for all ordinary, practical daily life. Without it you have a fair chance of losing your life as you cross a trafficky street! It is the isolativeness and separativeness of our self-consciousness – the love-and-life-destroying poison in any person's life – which utterly vanishes.

Hence the complete vanishing of the isolativeness and separativeness of self-consciousness is a priceless benefit, not only to yourself but also to your whole society and environment. This vanishing is one form of the realization of immortality whilst bodily alive. And then you can live and enjoy the Good Life in the supreme sense of the words 'enjoy' and 'Good'; that is, the life which is lived in complete relationship with Totality. Such is the godly life, the pure Zarathushtrian life, the Human life.

Such was the Wholeness *(Haurvatat)*, the Holiness, of Zarathushtra. Because of this realized Transcendence, Zarathushtra affirms positively: 'When I beheld thee in my very eyes' (Ys.31.8) This 'seeing with one's eyes' was one of the verbal forms used in the past by the Holy Ones to indicate their clear consciousness of Transcendence. This consciousness of the Holy Ones was the constant and enduring source of their teachings. The effect of the divine Revelation upon the mind, the secret of the religious practice culminating in the Vision of God, and the reiteration of the clear consciousness of God are affirmed thus: 'Now in truth have I beheld him clearly in my mind's eye. Knowing the perfect Mind, Word and Deed through Asha, I can now see Mazda Ahura himself.' (Ys.45.8)

Zarathushtra's teaching pre-eminently emphasizes and extols *asha*: purity (in thought and feeling, speech and action); the divine law and order; righteousness; virtue; truth.

Zarathushtra prays (Ys.31.5):
*Reveal unto me for my enlightenment that which through Asha
Thou has ordained as the better path for me to follow.*
And he declares (Ys.31.7,8):
He Himself (Ahura Mazda) is the Creator of Asha.
He questions (Ys.31.16):
*When the wise man.... strives earnestly for the increase of
Asha, would he then, by such action, become one with* (or, be
merged into) *Thee, O Mazda Ahura?*
He affirms (Ys.31.19):
*Whoso listens to and realizes Asha becomes the soul-healing
Lord of Wisdom, O Ahura.*

In verse 5 of Ys.31, Zarathushtra indicates, and in verse
19 confirms, that enlightenment dawns through *asha*, and
whoso realizes perfect Virtue becomes the soul-healing
Lord of Wisdom. Zarathushtra is the true 'psychotherapist'.
The enlightened Lord of Wisdom, the embodiment of
Virtue, whose soul is perfectly healthy, whose mind is
perfectly sane, is the one who can faultlessly diagnose the
psychical derangement of the sick and suffering worldling.
He is the 'psychotherapist' who can heal the unholy suf-
ferer. And he does it freely, for love's sake, in order that
divine grace be made manifest. Have we *such* 'psycho-
therapists' today? Only very few such Holy Ones. They are
not professionals. They do not make a living thereby – yet
they live their full life-span on 'manna from heaven'
serenely and healthily.

Because of the Wisdom and Compassion characterizing
their enlightened consciousness, the Holy Ones are chan-
nels for the Creative whole-making Power of Transcendence
which brings about Creative Renewal in the sick soul. And
so the 'blind' see and the 'lame' walk, and the 'deaf' hear
and the 'dumb' speak. And the one-time ailing man is
restored to hale human-ness.

The Holy One understands the sick psyche. He also
knows perfectly the pure psyche, which is unknown by the

worldly man however learned and well-trained he may be.
Himself being the pure human, he sees by direct insight
what is wrong with the deranged one. And he also knows
that he can heal those persons who approach him with faith.
Where there is faith there can be true repentance, an intelligent turning away from all that leads to and maintains the
sick state of the psyche. If a sick or tortured soul cares for
Truth, for Transcendence, with intense, calm passion, not
merely for his separate self but for all creation, then he is
one who will providentially be led to the great Healer.

Since Zarathushtra fully knew the holy state *(ashoi)* of the
psyche through his own realization and could function in
the supreme meditative state of the enlightened consciousness – witness his communion with Ahura Mazda, his
awakening to Sraosha (divine obedience, and obedience
means listening and responding to the Spirit), and his
affirmation that silent meditation is best for spiritual
enlightenment (Ys.43.12,15) – his teaching shows us the
Way to the culmination of man's evolving consciousness
and the Revelation of the Transcendent Infinite-Eternal,
the 'abode of Ahura Mazda' (see pages 17-19,27)

Verse 16 asks a question of deep import. It hints at the
deepest longing in the human spirit and also suggests the
Way. Can one be merged into or be united with God?
Could this happen for the *wise* man who strives earnestly
for the growth of *asha*? There is an implication here that the
growth of *asha* culminates in the supreme fulfilment of
godliness here and now in the world.

And indeed such fulfilment did take place. Zarathushtra
says (Ys.43.9):

*Then did I realize Thee as the Most Holy One, O Mazda Ahura,
when the Good Mind* (Vohu Manah, the divine Intelligence)
encircled me completely.

The affirmation 'encircled me completely' means that
Zarathushtra's whole being is suffused by that Archetypal

Energy, the Amesha Spenta named Vohu Manah, because of which divine Intelligence functions freely through him during his lifetime. The context of *vohu manah* is the transcendent context of the Infinite-Eternal. It subsumes the good thinking (*humata*, the good thought) of the wise man, the existential mortal living in the context of the finite and temporal. Since the Infinite-Eternal interpenetrates the finite and temporal there comes the time and circumstance when the mortal wakens to the Immortal.

How does this happen? Zarathushtra teaches positively (Ys.31.19): 'By *asha*'. By living the pure and righteous life in our finite world to the best of our ability, according to our own inner light and vision of the true and the good, the perceptiveness of our earnestly aspiring heart and intellect is stripped of all flaws and delusions. In this process, an extraordinary change takes place. Most of us observe a relative ethic: 'Friendliness and goodness from you will be reciprocated by me. If you harm me and continue to do so, I shall have to take steps against you.' But this relative ethic based on reciprocity is not the ethic of the purified and full-fledged Human, who lives by the transcendental ethic: 'Whatsoever you do to me, I shall always respond wisely with love and helpfulness.' This transformation is the extraordinary change which takes place by living according to *asha*. All true spiritual teachers, after their realization of perfect Holiness, lived by the transcendental ethic.

By such purification, the brain, freed of all its conditioning, is transformed, as it was in the case of Zarathushtra. And then, unerring sight into Truth (*baodha* and *daena*) characterizing the Pure Mind (*manangha*) functioned freely through Zarathushtra the finite mortal living in the world. The divine Intelligence, *Vohu Manah*, 'encircled him completely' and shone through him the Enlightened One. Thereafter, his Perfect Virtue (*Asha*) was the personal and earthly manifestation and counterpart of the divine Law and Order (*Asha*) of the Infinite-Eternal. And the effectiveness and victorious power *(Khshathra)* of the Prophet in the world was the expression of the majesty and Creative Energy *(Khshathra)* of Transcendence.

This is the stage which marks the flowering of the erstwhile wordly mortal into the Perfected Holy One, the true Human (the blissful wielder of the creative power of Mind which is untrammelled by any thinking or thought as manifested by us mortals). The consciousness of the Holy One is released out of duality's dolour and functions henceforth in the ineffable peace of unitary Wholeness. And the tongue of Revelation speaks the Holy Word emerging out of the silent depth of transcendent realization.

This Holy Word reveals man's divine heritage and potential; that within him Ahura Mazda is embodied, together with the Amesha Spentas, and that within his finite existential being lies the freedom to choose either the path of evil which leads to sorrow and suffering, or the path of Purity and Truth which spells *haurvatat* and *ameretat*. By the latter, he realizes his deepest and most direct relationship with Ahura Mazda who is Friend, Brother and Father (Ys.45.11). Such is his divine potential.

The importance of *asha* in the life and teachings of Zarathushtra cannot be overestimated. Again and again Zarathushtra invokes or speaks of *asha* throughout the Gathas. Asha (as well as a few words derived from *asha*) is mentioned in 73 out of 100 verses of the *Ahunavaiti Gatha*, 47 out of 66 in the *Ushtavaiti*, 34 out of 71 in the *Spenta Mainyu*, 17 out of 22 in the *Vohu Khshathtra*, and 5 out of 9 in the *Vahishta-Ishti;* that is, in 176 out of the 238 verses of all five Gathas.

God's name, in various forms such as Ahura or Mazda, as Ahura Mazda or Mazda Ahura, occurs right through the Gathas. And twice, Mazda Ahura, occurs in the plural (Ys.30.9. and Ys.31.4); then it stands for Ahura Mazda together with the six Amesha Spentas. Less than a score of the 238 verses do not mention the divine name. Of the

Amesha Spentas, Vohu Manah, in association with Asha, occurs more frequently than the other four.

Next to Vohu Manah comes Armaiti (God's transcendent Love for all Creation, man's supreme self-surrendering devotion to the divine). There are two most significant verses concerning Armaiti in the *Ahunavaiti* Gatha (Ys.34.9,10):

Those who, O Mazda, through ill-deeds and ignorance of Vohu Manah, scorn Holy Armaiti, revered by the enlightened Sage, from such she* completely withdraws together with Asha, even as we do from evil-doers.

But the Seer, knowing her* to be the ever-present core of Asha, speaks to these corrupt men of the inward essence of Vohu-Manah's workings. Through this knowledge, O Mazda, they will come again under Thy suzerainty, O Ahura.

'Armaiti the ever-present core of Asha'! Transcendent, constant Love, is the creative and inspiring power at the very heart of Truth and Goodness. Faithful devotion to immutable Law and Order reveals the divine Source of the moral imperative within us.

We know almost nothing about *asha*. This Law and Order is nothing imposed forcibly by an external autocrat. It is a power for harmony and for growing to fruition *inherent* in all Creation, from an atom to a cosmos, a microbe to a Perfected Holy One. Ahura Mazda *is asha*, is Law and Order, though we imperfect mortals see it not and live it not. So too, *transcendental* Love, *armaiti*, is something unknown by us, hardly ever expressed by us or functioning through us. Our type of love is attraction, attachment, bondage; the demand for sensational delight; a slavery to a violent and possessive pleasure drive; a precarious balancing of reciprocal demands and conditions, a bargaining. Very rarely is it the absolutely unconditional and unreser-

---

*Ahura is the Father aspect of God, Mazda the Mother aspect. Asha, Vohu Manah and Khshathra are neuter gender, and associated with Ahura. Armaiti, Haurvatat and Ameretat are feminine gender, and associated with Mazda.

ved total giving of one's whole self to the Beloved, asking
nothing, hoping or expecting nothing, in return. The idea
or consciousness of 'in return' is the evidence of disunity,
of the duality which poisons Love.

This transcendent Love cannot be cultivated. It is dormant within our existential being, the psycho-physical
organism which bears the name by which we are known in
the world. As and when our psyche is purified of all evil, of
all its illness, then this hidden transcendent energy of
universal, divine Love is no longer prevented from functioning in and through our finite, mortal being. Thus, that
which cannot be deliberately or desirously cultivated is
released into free functioning through us. Then *armaiti*
pervades all our life. We must remember that the Amesha
Spentas are archetypal forms operating universally on a
cosmic scale, of the primordial Creative Energy, the Infinite
Eternal Source. When this Energy functions in this way we
name it *asha*, in that way *Vohu Manah*, in still another way
armaiti, and so on. But in essence it is the One Energy, its
modes of manifestation display variety.

The purification of the psyche, cleansing it of wrath,
rapine, violence, greed, lust, fear, hate, stupidity, illusions
and delusions, is our special personal task. This cleansing
task is succinctly summed up in the Zarathushtrian teaching of *humata, hukhta, hvarshta* – good thoughts, good
words, good deeds – the correspondents at our individual
human level of *vohu-manah, asha* and *khshathra* in the
transcendent universal context. Whilst *armaiti* is declared
to be the ever-present or true core of *asha*, the release of
armaiti is the fruit of *asha's* activity in us. Thus we can
appreciate the statement by Ahura Mazda in answer to the
prayer by Zarathushtra and his disciples – and *also* by the
Daevas and the misinterpreters of the Truth (the *dregvants*,
the spawn of the Untruth as they are called in the Gathas) –
that they should become God's messengers and repel those
who were hostile to Ahura Mazda:

Close-knit to glorious Asha, Armaiti, the holy Guardian of your inmost faith, We choose for you both. (Ys.32.2)

There is here a remarkable implication of the forbearance and forgiveness of God in that he opens wide the door to redemption for good men as well as misguided wrong-doers. Add to this an assurance for the *dregvants* by Zarathushtra:

When retribution descends upon the sinners, then unto them O Mazda, will thy Law be clearly revealed by Vohu Manah, and unto them, O Ahura, shall teaching be given so that into the hands of Asha they will deliver up the false one.

When (retribution) destroys the (past) triumphs of the False ones, then they shall attain their inmost desire (namely, the innermost hidden longing for Ahura Mazda, hitherto suppressed by their misunderstanding of the Truth and by their misdeeds); they shall attain the Blessed Abode of Vohu Manah, of Mazda and of Asha.

So understand these Laws ordained by Mazda, O ye mortals, regarding happiness and pain: Falsehood brings age-long suffering whilst Truth leads to a fuller, higher life; then, after these, there shall be bliss. (Ys.30.8,10,11).

Zarathushtra declares (Ys.43.9,10):

I will esteem Asha above all as long as I am able. So do Thou guide me to Asha for whom I have ever yearned; fully loyal to Armaiti have I come.

And further (Ys.43.16):

Thus, O Ahura Mazda, Zarathushtra chooses for himself Thy Spirit which indeed is holiest. May Asha incarnate in us, filling our living being with Thy Life and Strength. May Armaiti dwell with Khshathra in sunlike splendour and bestow blessings for deeds inspired by Vohu Manah.

The quintessence of Zarathushtra's teaching, as stated earlier, is contained in that one word *asha*. Each one of the Amesha Spentas has been càlled 'Lord of *asha*'. The foundation stone of our whole life is *asha*. And, in the later Avestan texts, devout worshippers express the wish (Ys.60.12):

Through the best Asha, through the highest Asha, may we obtain a vision of Thee, may we draw near unto Thee, and may we be in perfect union with Thee.

And Yasna 71.11 affirms:

There is only one Path, the Path of Asha; all others are false paths.

In the Gathas, Ahura Mazda, the living God of all Creation and Life is said to be 'of one accord with *asha*' (Ys.28.8).

What is the fruit of the realization and fulfilment of *asha*?

Unto him, who (moved by the call of the) Holy Spirit and the Divine Mind, expresses Asha in deed and word, will Ahura Mazda, through his Khshathra and through Armaiti, bestow haurvatat (supreme well-being) and ameretat (immortality). (Ys.47.1)

Such is the culmination of each individual's development, not only for a Zarathushtrian but also for any man or woman in all the wide world. It is necessary for us to understand quite clearly and rationally the meaning of supreme well-being and of immortality.

When the heart is morally pure, free of evil desires*, passions, malevolence, reactions of hate and ill-will, and feelings of envy, jealousy and greed, and all craving for the gratification of sensuous urges in all their subtle forms – when the brain is calm, poised, alert and observant, free of

*And ultimately of *all* desire, good and bad alike; for desire even when good is self-oriented. When every desire is out, the Infinite-Eternal sweetly and beautifully expresses itself through us.

bias, prejudices, preconceptions and unwarranted assumptions, of rigid mental fixations, of fear and anxiety, stupidity and obstinacy, of confusion and restlessness, of vanity, egoism, self-conceit and self-centredness – when the feminine elements in the psyche are in harmony with the natural masculinity in a man, and the masculine elements in the psyche are in harmony with the natural femininity in a woman – and when the body is at ease, well-coordinated, free of disease, functioning and acting rhythmically – then indeed that person enjoys the state of perfect well-being. He is self-reliant, has peace of mind, is skilled in action and is in right relationship with all people and with his environment.

(Page43)

4

Immortality

Some religions promise blissful immortality after death in an eternal heaven to the faithful devotee who has lived the Good Life, and consign unrepentant sinners to everlasting tortures in a permanent hell.

Religions which uphold theories of karma and rebirth teach that, after the effects of all the causes generated by each human being have worked themselves out through many lives on earth – during which he has at last turned his face to the Light and succeeded in realizing perfection and has fully awakened to Truth – man will then be one with the Ultimate Reality, or be united with God, or enjoy everlasting fellowship with God, perpetually standing in the Divine Presence. Heaven, Nirvana, Paradise, Garo-demana, the Happy Lands, etc., will be the reward, a final payment, for him as an individual, self-conscious being.

Man is in thrall to duality. Credit and debit, success and failure, gain and loss, reward and punishment, pleasure and pain – all these duals dominate his deeds, misguide his mind and lead him astray. Being isolatively self-conscious, it is difficult for him to walk out of his ego-centred prison – self-condemned to hard labour which brings only conflict and insecurity, misery and despair, not only to him but also those around him. Such is man who is still in his sub-human stage of development. And yet, this self-same creature, man, is indeed Transcendence embodied, bearing within himself a wonderful spiritual heritage and a divine potential. (See pp.26,27.)

Founders of religions have been credited by their followers with being sons of God, as with Zarathushtra and

Jesus, or as being God incarnate, as with Shree Krishna. As such, omniscience has been ascribed to them, just as it has been ascribed to Gotama the Buddha. The masses imagine that this omniscience is an encyclopedic knowledge of the whole cosmos, including man, and all its past, present and future, as also of celestial realms invisible to us ordinary people.

All true spiritual teachers thoroughly understand the human psyche. Compared with us, they are omniscient in this sphere. They are 'soul-healing Lords of Wisdom'. By the complete understanding and purification and the consequent healing of their own psyches, they become eminently qualified to diagnose the illness of any soul and to suggest the right remedy. Their prescription is always a suggestion, never a compulsion. If the patient is sensible, he will do the needful. If not, the consequences will be his.

Such spiritual teachers were living examples of the apothegm *mens sana in corpore sano*, a healthy mind in a healthy body, which is one meaning of *haurvatat*. They well knew the power of the healthy psyche to heal, through *asha*, the entire psycho-physical existential being and maintain him in perfect health, so that the person could duly realize his spiritual goal. Here lies the significance of the later Avestan prayers in oft-repeated phrases like:

O Lord God, Ahura Mazda, from all my sins do I repent and turn back. From every evil thought, evil word and evil deed, which in this world I may have conceived of, uttered or committed, which from me has come forth, or originated through me; of all such sins of thought, word and deed, pertaining to my body or soul, pertaining to this world or the spiritual world; O Lord! with sincere contrition I repent with three-fold renunciation.

By the accomplished turning away from all evil, the person becomes the New Man.

The Holy Ones clearly understood the ambivalence of the

psyche, its relationship to and interaction with one's innermost consciousness which is not cognized by the brain. This consciousness is the silent watcher and lord, sustainer and consummator of our entire existential being, the microcosm. It does not depend upon sense activity, concept and word for its operation. It is a constant, tranquil influence for the purification and well-being of the psycho-physical person. It is non-compulsive in its action, neither persuading nor dissuading. It is universal. It is Transcendence embodied in us, and is not to be mistaken for the ordinary discriminative consciousness (which does depend upon sense activity, concept and word) characterizing the everyday living process of our psycho-physical organism.

Because of its ambivalence, the psyche injects both good and evil influences into the psychical atmosphere. The psyche also draws upon and is affected by the accumulated store of good and evil psychical energy enveloping the world, like the pure as well as the polluted air which encloses the earth and which we all breathe. Whereas we usually have little choice where the quality of the air we breathe is concerned, we do have considerable freedom of choice where the psychical atmosphere is concerned, for this depends upon what company we keep, upon our cultural and spiritual interests and upon being aware of our own psychological states.

Here we must consider an important teaching of Zarathushtra, namely, his doctrine of the twin *mainyu* – the twin spirits or twin powers, the one promoting and the other spoiling or destroying well-being and the purpose of existence.

In his very first sermon, Zarathushtra says to the assembled people:

Now to the eagér ones I will speak of the Two created by Mazda – this is for the wise. (Ys.30.1)

Here the Two are not specified. Zarathushtra continues:

(I shall sing) hymns unto Ahura and the praises of Vohu Manah; (and explain) the sacred lore of Asha also, so that you may attain perfection in realms of light.

In the next verse he exhorts the people:

Give ear to the highest (truths). *Let each one, man by man, consider them with an illumined mind, before deciding for himself which of two paths he decides to tread. Wake up each one of you and spread this* (message) *before the great ushering of the New Age* (of the worship of the One God, Ahura Mazda). (Ys.30.2)

In the third verse he states the nature of the twin spirits. They are co-workers, but they are opposed in thought, word and deed. The 'good' twin (as stated in the fourth verse) generates life and promotes spiritual growth, whilst the 'bad' twin is the agent of dissolution.

One may wonder why Ahura Mazda should produce a good and also a bad spirit – two opposite energies. Any manifestation, material or biological or cultural, requires the stimulus, challenge and friction caused by contrasting energy; intellectual and aesthetic development, and moral and spiritual advancement is promoted thereby. If a person was deprived of the activity of the inferior, of the less good (the 'bad') and its consequences, he would remain lacking in true discernment. This does not mean that he himself must deliberately do evil. He himself needs to observe evil done around him by those who are immature enough to indulge in it, and thereby learn how to live in accord with *asha*. Therefore Zarathushtra categorically states: 'Thus it is that Creation's purpose is fulfilled.'

All Perfected Holy Ones know that God is inconceivable and indescribable by us at our present level. God creates. This means that the primordial, undifferentiated Creative Energy is stirred out of its vibrant, quiescent state and the Cosmos comes into being – Manifestation in an infinite variety of forms. All Creation is an existence – a standing

out of (*ex* + *sistere*, to stand) the One Source. Activity,
movement, form, shape, change, life and death, always
involve the constant interaction of the complementary
opposites composing all duality. Without the operation of
such duality there could be no existence, no manifestation
of God.

Since all manifestation is a dynamic process of constant
change, there is the perpetual interaction of what we call
good and evil, construction and dissolution, positive and
negative, male and female. All existence is of and in God,
but God is not confined to existence. God is. Though God is
unknown and unknowable, we can see and touch and
know a small portion of Manifestation (the reflection of
God projected out of God by God's own magic play, *maya*),
and grow in virtue (*asha*) and realize God's, and our own,
perfect humanity, human godliness.

All existence tends this way, yearning towards its
specific perfection – the gem, the flower, the thorn, the
tree, the ant, the viper, the Holy One, the angel, the
demon, *ad infinitum*. God that is remains, for us, the
Mystery. Does God, seeing God's divine signature
throughout the pulsating immensity – all existence – ever
know God? God knows. Or, maybe, God does not care to
know. Mystery! Wondrous Mystery! Be reverent by
letting the Mystery be. Such is the Way of Purity, and
Wisdom and Love, of *asha* and *vohu manah* and *armaiti*.
And by treading that Way, Creation's purpose for man is
fulfilled.

That is what Zarathushtra teaches. Man is free to choose
his path. The Creative Energy functions in terms of duality,
giving rise to *gaya* on the one hand – life, growth and
fulfilment – and to *ajyaiti* on the other – degeneration,
decay and dissolution – which is a transformation process
leading to a different kind of existence. Zarathushtra
unequivocally extols and upholds Truth and exhorts man to
live in accordance with it. He himself is its shining Exemplar.

Whoso lives thus realizes *haurvatat*, supreme well-being, and *ameretat*, immortality.

In the next chapter, he says:

Since, O Mazda, from the beginning Thou didst fashion for us physical bodies, discerning souls and directive Intelligences through Thy own Mind; since Thou didst infuse life into the body, grant us capacities to act and true doctrines to guide so that one could hold whatever faith one wills.

Therefore each one loudly announces his belief, be he speaking incorrectly or truly, be he enlightened or unenlightened; but Armaiti, standing ever close, appeals to the heart and head of each one through his spirit, to resolve his doubts. (Ys.31.11,12)

It rests with each man to make the right choice. Should he do so, Sraosha (from the root *sru*, to hear), divine obedience, stirs into action within him and guides him. Armaiti's ministrations are largely responsible for stirring Sraosha into action, for where there is that devotion which naturally and spontaneously moves the heart of love to Transcendence Itself, it becomes easy to listen to the inner voice. Obedience (*ob* + *audire*, to hear) basically means 'to give ear to', to hearken. And it is noteworthy how Zarathushtra emphasizes this meaning:

Give ear to the Highest. (Ys.30.2)

Who giveth ear to and realizes asha becomes the soul-healing Lord of Wisdom, O Ahura. To spread true teaching he becomes capable and eloquent of tongue. (Ys.31.19)

Hearken now with your ear. Listen to me all ye who have come from far and near, yearning to know. (Ys.45.1)

The implication associated with such hearing or listening is that the listener will seriously reflect upon what he hears, and translate it into action out of his free choice.

This, and not a thoughtless or unwilling conforming out of fear to a forcible imposition, is true obedience.

In this inward spiritual listening, no words in any language are heard. If the attentiveness is intense and the brain is alert and quiet, free of the endless inaudible chatter which is its usual state of turmoil, the mode of awareness undergoes a transformation, giving rise to deep insights rather than spasmodic intuitive flashes. This transformation can affect the psycho-physical organism favourably and subsequently give rise to illuminating concepts clothed in appropriate and telling verbal formulations. The intellectual clear-sightedness of enlightened consciousness often finds powerful, poetic expression. Very significantly, the great scriptures of the world are couched in poetic language, uplifting and inspiring. Truth and Beauty are close companions.

Our usual mode of awareness – as I have propounded earlier – is the mode of finitude, temporality and mortality. Living the religious life as taught by the Holy Ones transforms this mode of awareness. Consciousness evolves, becoming increasingly free of separativeness and isolativeness, and culminates in awareness in the mode of unitary Wholeness. Ordinarily, we are conscious in terms of beginning-proceeding-ending – the usual birth-death process of successive events in our lives – and of our mental states, and of our own psycho-physical organism. Whatever begins or is born at some instant ends or dies afterwards. Something else then begins and also ends. Between the end of one and the beginning of another there is a gap and a break in consciousness. These recurrent breaks in our consciousness throughout our lifetime is one meaning of being aware in the mode of mortality. When there is a break in consciousness we cease to attend, and any cessation of attentiveness produces a break in consciousness.

If there is no disjunction in attentiveness, constant wakefulness prevails. Thus, by going beyond awareness in the mode of mortality, the deathless state is present and the immortal is realized in consciousness. If this happens to you, it does not mean that the psycho-physical organism will continue to live for ever. The organism, like all matter (whether gross or subtle, corpuscular or radiant), is bound within the constraints of space-time, the context of finitude and temporality and the inexorability of change, of beginning or birth and ending or death. The passing away into non-being of whatever comes into being is indeed ineluctable. So, the realization of immortality whilst the deathless state prevails through your organism is limited to your experience of timelessness bounded by two points in time, namely, the moments of immergence into and emergence out of that state.

It is, however, not exclusively yours. For, in that state of deathlessness, the context in which your consciousness functions is the context of the Infinite-Eternal, which (as described in Ch. 2) fully subsumes and wholly interpenetrates the finite, temporal and hence mortal context in which your psycho-physical organism subsists. As a particular individual in that state you are wholly integrated into the One Total Reality. But the existence of your living psycho-physical organism compulsively re-imposes the limitations of finitude and temporality – the body *has* to feed, eliminate, sleep, etc. – upon that transcendent state and you 'come back' to your organic state and discriminative consciousness. If you did not come back, the psycho-physical organism – you, the person known in the world – would die.

Actual Immortality transcends both time and timelessness. It is identical with Eternity. Therefore, whilst you can consciously 'touch' the deathless state and enter the infinity of all manifestation, no 'you' as a particular individual entity can BE immortal, BE eternal. We can, nevertheless, simply, humbly and quietly affirm the Immortal, the Eternal, if we do experience the deathless state.

Transcendence, the Infinite-Eternal, the Immortal, is

totally embodied in the whole cosmos. It is as if it were materialized as every thing and every creature. It exists as countless 'beings'. When fulfilled, there is the dissolution of being-ness, and countless beings are ultimately the one and only non-being. Transcendence is the absolute all. God is verily God, inscrutable. The smile on the face of the inscrutable remains the Mystery. Do not probe. 'Tis immodest to do so. Veil your face and look down. The Infinite-Eternal will lift that veil and see you. *You* will never see or know. You could, however, fly straight into the heart of Mystery. This is LOVE.

Whilst absorbed in timelessness during the deathless state, Immortality is that fusion in consciousness with the Infinite-Eternal in which there is the total disappearance of isolative separate self-consciousness. There is no constant immortality for any entity-being. All raindrops are divested of their separate identity when they fall into the river, as do all rivers when they meet the ocean. Every entity-being is finite and mortal, and totally ceases to be an identifiable entity after death. Whilst living, that organism was Transcendence embodied. At death, that Transcendence is just Transcendence, the One Absolute Reality. The consciousness of any being is isolative and discriminative, inevitably producing separation, fragmentation and disunity – the unwholeness which is unholiness. When and whilst the deathless state prevails through your *asha, vohu manah* and *armaiti*, the Pure Consciousness of Unitary Wholeness in you is awake, one with the Absolute Consciousness of Transcendence, which is Immortality.

Such is the nature of Zarathushtra's teaching. The fruition of life for the human being is the actualizing in consciousness of the Absolute Silence, the ultimate NO-THING (not nothing, but NO-THING which is God). Such is the glorification of the sinless full-fledged human. It is also the liberation of Transcendence out of Its self-imposed imprisonment in the finitude and temporality of Its fleshly existence. Man is the child of God. God loves the child. Let man realize love for God. Thus he becomes indispensable to God and well remembers that God is not an absolute Other beyond an unbridgeable chasm, for he himself, man, is God voluntarily self-restricted.

Recall now Zarathushtra's teaching regarding the Silence:

Then did I realize Thee as the most Bountiful One, O Mazda Ahura, when the Good Mind encircled me completely. He declared to me that silent meditation is the best for attaining spiritual enlightenment. (Ys.43.15)

The common, worldly meaning of meditating is musing, ruminating, thinking quietly about a problem or a particular subject, secular or spiritual. Discursive thinking is inaudible talking, involving the concentration of attention upon the subject under consideration. The quieter one is, the more intellectually clarifying and fruitful is the thinking. But all talking, audible or inaudible, is confined to the context of the finite and temporal, the sphere of mortality – when one *thinks* or *talks about* the Transcendent – because one is still actually conscious only in the worldly mode of separativeness and isolativeness. If one remains completely calm, *effortlessly*, the brain stops talking, the turbulent flow of discursive thinking comes to an end, and the mode of awareness is transformed into that of the Infinite and ever-present Now.

This ending of discursive thought and the transformation of consciousness spell the pacification (*not* the suppression) of all the sense functions. In fact, the senses function with intensely heightened sensitivity and the utmost receptivity to divine influences never sensed before, because now they are unhindered, unspoilt, by the brain's naming process, which, being analytical, splits up the wholeness. Indeed, the senses are now the cords of Communion.

Isolative self-consciousness vanishes, the wound of separation between subject and object, observer and observed, is healed, and unitary wholeness is clearly revealed through Creative Action in Unity Consciousness. This timeless conjugation is the pure meditative state – silent meditation – a state of ineffable peace and of creative activity impossible to describe, impossible to represent in any humanly expressive terms. When you Love transcendentally, the words 'I love you' are pathetically nugatory.

Zarathushtra does not expound in detail his solitary statement (quoted above) regarding meditation. Just as at our finite level the solution of a philosophical or scientific problem brings intellectual enlightenment, so too silent meditation spells spiritual enlightenment, but not in our worldly, mortal mode of awareness. Intellectual perception, and ordinary sense functioning and thinking, are transcended. Consciousness is no longer discriminative – analytical, separative and isolative. It is at home in the context of the Infinite and Eternal, functioning as unitary wholeness. In simple terms, Zarathushtra and Ahura Mazda, man and God, are one. The fusion in Consciousness has taken place. Thereupon, consciousness in terms of succession, that is, of a beginning followed by an ending, followed by another beginning and its ending, repeatedly, gives place to a whole awareness of pure change.

Pure change is life dying into new life. The previous emerges into the present. If you are totally attentive, death is 'faded out' of the situation. One may say, 'not death but life is faded out of the situation.' Not so, for since the 'was' has become the 'is now', Life has transformed into Other-Life. Pure change is a Life/Other-Life and not a Life/Death pulse. What seems to us to be Death, is only another mode of Livingness, but not as the previous identifiable entity. Just as a permanent magnet has a north pole and a south pole, Life in its integral wholeness has a positive expression, of which we finite mortals are conscious, and also a hidden expression of which we are normally unconscious. They are the complementary components of Life Eternal.

So, in this fusion of Consciousness, there is no break in consciousness as with consciousness in the mode of mortality. Consciousness of 'otherness' vanishes. Also, there is no continuity, for time has been transcended. There is the simultaneity of what used to be experienced as birth *followed* by death. There is only the immediacy of the Creative Action of Eternal Life. Time and its sorrow and pleasure (duality), timelessness and its enstasy (non-duality) are transcended through their integration into Eternity – integration, not mere synthesis (which is mechanical).

At the same time, there is no annihiliation of discriminative consciousness, indispensable for the organsim living in the world. If it were annihiliated, the Transcendent Unitary Consciousness could no longer subsume discriminative consciousness functioning in the mode of mortality. In which case, there would be an unbridgeable gulf between man and God, between the limitation and bondage of manifestation (Appearance) and the freedom of Transcendence (Ultimate Reality). The Holy One's Consciousness can function freely in the mode of mortality and in the mode of immortality, as and when required.

The fusion in consciousness is the realization of Immortality. Ahura Mazda (God, Godhead, Brahman or whatever name you like to use) is the Eternal Immortal. For Zara-thushtra, whilst he is bodily alive – and so too for any Perfected Holy One during his earthly life-span – this Transcendent Consciousness of Immortality into which he can enter again and again when he needs to, remains as a permanent background in his being. It is a constant source of divine creative power – *khshathra* – animating and sustaining his mission in the world; of divine wisdom – *vohu manah* – inspiring his teaching; of transcendental ethic – *asha* – a purifying Fire of Life releasing that moral imperative deep-seated in one's soul which helps one to live the Holy Life at all times and in all places; of that love of

God – *armaiti* – which heals all sorrow and transmutes all evil; and of that supreme well-being and immortality – *haurvatat* and *ameretat* – the crowning fulfilment of man. It makes *sraosha* – 'giving ear to and obeying God' – a factual reality in one's life.

And when this earthly life ends, the complete and perfect death of this existential being spells the release of the embodied Transcendence out of Its self-imposed constriction. This is how the existential human being proves his indispensability to God. No finite mortal liberates himself – he can only liberate the embodied Transcendence by his flowering into the full-fledged perfect Human. Every flower – the existential shape and form – soon withers and dies. Its perfume gladdens man and the world and lives deathlessly as a happy memory.

Never crave, then, for your separate personal perpetuity – a tragic trapping in time's tormenting tentacles. Do not fear death of the body, but like the sere leaf ready to dance its ecstatic return into the bosom of mother earth, silently and peacefully greet that supremely divine moment when the Infinite Eternal will bless you for your perfect selfless service towards effecting Its own release out of the bonds of existence.

THOU art Immortal. THOU art *ahmi*, the eternal I AM*.

Sing, O Heavenly Bird! Sing praise to the Lord of Life and Wisdom for sending sweet Death to heal all my ill and to open the door to His own Immortality.

---

*Ahuramazda Yasht, para. 13.

5

Some Untenable Doctrines

A critical reader might say that part of the exposition in the previous three chapters – and the meaning given to such terms as Transcendence, God, Primordial Creative Energy, Consciousness, Infinity, Eternity and Immortality – are foreign to the recorded traditional teachings of Zarathush-trianism. So they are. In fact they are foreign to the traditional teachings of most of the established religions of the world.

Readers who are fundamentalists will, understandably, reject out of hand various statements presenting such concepts as:

Immortality can be experienced in the *Unio Mystica* whilst bodily alive (pp.51,55);

Consciousness in culmination is made manifest as Perfect Action, which is a 'knowing by being or doing' that of which one was partially and isolatively conscious (p.17)

Man is Transcendence embodied;

The whole of Transcendence and the whole of Infinity and all Eternity completely subsume and fully interpenetrate every single particular, however minute or however large, throughout the whole cosmos (p.18).

Before the developments in science and psychology during the last century or two, such concepts could not have been formulated. But now they are appropriate for our own day and age. They contradict some ancient fixed beliefs cherished by many people. But cherished fixations ultimately disappear as and when understanding deepens and vision is clearer. Doubtless, it seems rank heresy to contradict firmly established scriptural beliefs. But did not all the Teachers of the past contradict some of the authoritative dogmas prevalent in their day? Were they not regarded as heretics?

Consider the opposition to Zarathushtra by the *karapans* and *kavayas* (Ys.46.11), by the False Teachers – the followers of the Druj who 'corrupt the course of our life' (Ys.32.11) – or by Bendva (Ys.49.1,2). Consider the enmity of the Jews and their high priests, Caiaphas and Annas, against Jesus Christ, of the Meccans against Muhammed and the Muslims against al-Hallaj. A new vision or revelation may be called a heresy when it is first affirmed. Sooner or later it becomes the accepted truth when people have outgrown the old belief and have advanced to a clearer understanding.

Ceaseless change outstandingly characterizes the whole evolutionary process. If the change is progressive – and not fortuitous or regressive or destructive – it brings us nearer to fruition in all respects. Truth itself is usually postulated as being immutable; but its perception and formulation depend upon and are limited by level of development. Of necessity, that perception and formulation undergo changes in accordance with greater enlightenment in consciousness. With continuous investigation, fresh discoveries are made which lead to clearer understanding of the subject in hand. This requires a more fitting description than the old one. Sometimes one has only to reformulate the old one in clearer terms; at other times to contradict some aspect of it; occasionally, to supplant it altogether.

There are certain teachings and beliefs in all religions which need critical examination.

First let us consider the doctrines of eternal heaven for the good-doer and eternal hell for the evil-doer after death – in accordance with the fiat of the Divine Justiciar. Zarathushtra says in his Gathas:

O ye mortals, know and learn the Laws of Happiness and

Misery which Mazda has ordained for you. Age-long suffering for the followers of Falsehood, but a fuller, higher life for the upholders of Truth. (Ys.30.11)

For those who do not live according to Mazda's Holy Word as I expound it, the only end of life is woe. (Ys.45.3)

To those who offer obedience and reverence to Mazda's Holy Word shall come Perfection and Immortality, and also Mazda Ahura Himself, through deeds inspired by Vohu Manah. (Ys.45.5)

Thou hast ordained through Thy Wisdom that all deeds and words shall bear fruit – evil to the evil-doer, good blessings to him who does good, till the end of time. (Ys.43.5)

When the priests and princes who follow Falsehood come to Thy Judgment Bridge, for all time they shall dwell in the abode of Untruth (hell). (Ys.46.11)

Through his Holy Spirit and Divine Mind, Mazda Ahura will grant Perfection and Immortality to him whose deeds are in harmony with Asha. (Ys.47.1)*

Texts of the later Avestan period (c. 800 BC to AD 200), and particularly of the Pahlavi period (3rd to the 9th century AD), actually located and described heaven and hell. For three nights after death the soul stays near the person's head. Then at dawn after the third night, the soul approaches the *chinvato peretu* (Vd.19.29), the bridge of the Divider, the Judgment Bridge. Mithra presides there; Rashnu, who holds the scales of Justice, and Sraosha are also there. The bridge, which begins from the heights of the Elburz mountains, joins this world with the other world. Angels (Yt.22.25) and spiritual hounds (Vd.13.9; cf. the Greek Cerberus and the Vedic Sarama) guard the bridge which becomes broad and easy to traverse by the pious faithful –

---

*Similar statements are made in Ys.31.6.20;32.15;45.7,10;46.19;51.14.

who are helped by the angels and hounds (Vd.19.30) – but becomes razor-edged for the wicked. The pious go upward to heaven which is beautiful, magnificent, full of light. The highest heaven is Garo-Demana, the House of Song, Ahura Mazda's favourite residence (Vd.19.30; 22.1). Vohu Manah, the Holy Immortal, welcomes the soul on its first entry into heaven (Vd.19.31). Rejoicing, the soul then goes on to Ahura-Mazda Himself and the Amesha-Spentas (Vd.19.32) in Garo-Demana, and lives there in perfect peace, constantly chanting the Avesta. Ambrosia and nectar refresh the pious soul.

The impious soul falls down into hell from the Judgment Bridge. Here, the Evil Spirit, Angra Mainyu, dwells in darkness. Foul is the food and speech in hell, and the wind has a horrible stench. Hell is full of hideousness and terror (Vd.13.8; 4.49-55) and terrible are the torments to be endured. No escape is possible. There is a mid-region for souls whose good and evil deeds exactly balance each other.

The Christian picture of life after death is depicted by the poetic genius of Dante in his *Divina Commedia*, in three sections – *Inferno*, *Purgatorio* and *Paradiso*. The profound mysticism and the aesthetic perfection of *Paradiso* touched supremely exalted heights of transcendent states. But the tortures of hell described in the *Inferno* are as horrible and absurd as those depicted in all other religions.

The teaching of Muhammed in the Quran also affirms the everlasting nature of heaven and hell in the after-death state.

Hinduism and Buddhism hold the doctrines of karma and rebirth. The ultimate end after innumerable lives, is transcendent bliss. But during this vast aeonian span, heaven is experienced for meritorious deeds on earth, and hell for evil-doing.

All those who have written of the joys of heaven and the torments of hell have given free rein to their imagination, exercising neither judicious restraint nor good sense.

Others have portrayed these joys and torments in frescoes on temple walls or sculptures.

We must question these teachings and beliefs about heavenly felicities and hellish woes.

First, how can any mortal human, finite and limited in his abilities and powers, live in such a manner as to give rise to an infinite and unlimited consequence such as a heaven or hell for all time? Obviously, it is impossible – unless a human being of infinite ability and power arose, whose infinite righteousness or infinite evil were able to give rise to an infinite consequence. But such a man would have to be God or the very Devil! So this case cannot occur. Moreover, right-doing or wrong-doing by the limited human is measurable. Right-doing can range from saintly action to common decency; wrong-doing from a petty peccadillo to fiendish cruelty. They all belong to the context of the finite and temporal, and their consequences also belong to that limited, measurable context. The infinite and eternal are immeasurable. Thus there can be no eternal hell or heaven for any mortal after death.

Next consider the descriptions of these joys and sorrows. They are of the earth earthy. In the scriptures of the Pahlavi period, many centuries after the death of Zarathushtra, we are told that the souls of the pious are happy and glorious, deathless and untroubled, and enjoy fragrant breezes sweet as the basil (Mkh.7.13-17; 40.30). Radiant like the stars above, they sit on golden thrones and carpets (AV.7.2,3; 8.7; 9.3,4). It is also said that these good souls are clothed in garments embroidered with gold and silver. They sit on richly adorned cushions, those of women being bedecked with jewellery and those of warriors with golden arms and equipment studded with jewels (Mkh.2.154,156. AV.12.2,3,7,9,14,16; 13.1,2; 14.7-9,14; 15.9). The pious enjoy the same food in heaven as the angels, ambrosia; they enjoy happiness and remain full of glory till the day of Resurrection (Mkh.2.152,156,157; 7.17; 40.30; Dd.31.25).

Such descriptions were given by Arda Viraf, who was regarded as one of the most righteous and saintly priests in the reign of King Shabuhr the Second (AD 307-379). That king desired to obtain a description of the state of the souls in the other world by one who could enter it in trance and afterwards give an account of what he saw there. After various ceremonies, Arda Viraf himself partook of some consecrated wine and entered into a trance lasting seven days and nights during which his soul visited heaven and hell. On awakening out of his trance he described his visions, of which some account of souls in heaven has been given above. The state in hell is the counterpart, in terms of horror and torment, of the heavenly state.

Many centuries earlier Zarathushtra himself had given no such descriptions. He had, quite simply, affirmed the Laws of Life.

How can we possibly accept the kind of statements made by Arda Viraf, or by Dante in his *Inferno*, or by anyone else, as true facts. The soul is postulated as immortal. The context of the immortal is the immaterial, the infinite and the eternal. In the after-death state (if there is one), there is obviously a complete absence of everything material – clothes, thrones, gold, perfumed breezes, and all the pleasures and torments which a living person on earth experiences. Whilst we are alive we do experience serene and blissful states of mind, and also lacerations of the heart, painful bodily illnesses and mental disorders. But is it not absurd to transpose anything that characterizes finite and temporal materiality into the context of infinite and eternal immateriality? And surely, to locate heaven and hell above and below the Elburz mountains, to ascribe temperatures to them, and to indulge in materialistic descriptions of them, is altogether nonsensical.

'Heaven' and 'hell' are our psychological and physical states here and now whilst the body lives.

What we call 'body' is actually the Whole Reality –

material body, psyche, spirit – all subsisting as a Unitary Organism which is Transcendence embodied. What is called material, finite and mortal, and what is called immaterial, eternal and immortal – all these in their integrated wholeness constitute the living body, the individual man who is veritably the microcosm, the miniature cosmos representing the macrocosm, the One Total Reality. This 'body' is sacred. Hence Zarathushtra's emphasis on purity of body, and the many Zarathushtrian ritualistic daily observances in connection with bodily purity.

In the soil of environment, the body is the tree on which there can flower the blossoms of transcendent Love and Wisdom, of Intelligence which is unerring Insight into Truth, and of Vision which sees Ahura-Mazda with its very eyes – even as Zarathushtra did. *This* is your Highest Heaven, your *Garo-demana*. For you will sing the song of Eternal Life which is far beyond any chanting of any Scripture, even the Holy Avesta. Therefore, never abuse the body in any way whatsoever. Revere it as the Temple of the Most High.

Spenta Mainyu, the beneficent spirit, and Angra Mainyu, the hurtful troublesome Spirit, are both operative in the psycho-physical organism. Zarathushtra teaches that we are free to choose. This is a questionable statement. For vast numbers of people in the world, environment is such a frustrating power that they are incapable of exercising free choice. They never realize that hidden within them, perhaps too deeply, is an element at least of a moral imperative which is derived from a transcendent source – Asha as Zarathustra taught, Rita as the Rig-veda put it. But let them put faith in it – if only as an experiment – even once, with sincerity – and they will witness a miracle. The divine power for good of *'Behram yazad, pirozhgar dushman jadar,'* the Angel Behram, victorious conqueror of the enemy, will rise in invincible might and put them in the ranks of those who serve Spenta Mainyu, Mazda's Holy Spirit.

So when we do right in accord with *asha*, Spenta Mainyu in us is operative and we experience a 'reward', always spiritually and sometimes physically also – an agreeable, happy, healthy state psycho-physically, together with worldly benefits occasionally. When we do wrong by going against *asha*, Angra Mainyu is operative and we experience a 'punishment' – a disagreeable, miserable, diseased state, psycho-physically. We experience the inevitable consequences of our thoughts, words and deeds according to the inexorable Laws of Life as Zarathustra taught when he declared 'the worst life for the followers of Untruth, but the beatific state for the follower of Truth' (Ys.30.4) and that 'each man shall act in full accord with these principles which are the Primal Laws of Life' (Ys.33.1). Thus is worked out what Hinduism and Buddhism call the Law of Karma, and Zarathushtra called the Primal Laws of Life.

Hinduism and Buddhism taught that karma is fully worked out through an immense number of reincarnations, and strict justice is done. Zarathushtrianism, like Christianity and Islam, talks of the perfect justice of God in terms of a single lifetime on earth, followed by heaven or hell for all time. For Zarathushtra, time ends at the Resurrection. Justice is thought of in all religions in terms of reward and punishment – a sad misconception. Neither karma nor Divine Justice is concerned with paying out rewards or inflicting punishments like a benign boss or a stern schoolmaster.

The whole of the karmic process, of Divine Justice, functions in order to *heal*, to make whole, perfect, Holy. Probably the best definition of justice in past ages was given by Aristotle in his *Nicomachean Ethics* (Bk.5, Chap.2). Briefly stated: 'Justice is the practice of perfect Virtue to all others and to oneself.' Perfect Virtue – *asha*! Aristotle also says: 'The violator of the Law is unjust and the keeper of the Law is just.'

If we translate this into Zarathushtrian terms, justice, as

the practice of Perfect Virtue to all without exception, would mean living in thought and word and deed in accord with *asha* the Divine Law. It is insufficiently appreciated that this law operates ceaselessly and instantaneously, so that, whilst we are alive on earth, everything works out naturally. Every thought, word and deed is associated with electrochemical changes in the body. Each change, the consequence, is usually very small, because of the small-ness of the physical or psychical energy which caused the change. The process takes place so rapidly that we cannot keep track of it. There is no left-over to be worked out after death.

But this must not be regarded as permission for moral *laissez-faire*. Fools and the evil-minded have always flung morality to the winds undeterred by the fear or threat of hell after death. But the wise will understand this rightly. They will realize Truth, peace of mind and spiritual Bea-titude here and now – and thereby an extraordinary freedom from fear and anxiety – a blissful state.

When the body – which is the nexus of coherence for all else that constitutes the 'self' – dies, all else disappears with it, for every energy, spiritual or material, needs its appro-priate apparatus to manifest itself and its properties. No named item composing the 'all else' is a particular, measur-able, separate, identifiable entity. It is all the One Creative Energy, functioning in different ways, ensouling and animating everything there is in all existence. It is named in various ways, such as Archangels, Angels, Spirits, bodies, etc., *ad infinitum*. The Infinite-Eternal is released out of the bonds of existence on the dissolution of its material mode of manifestation – on the death of the body. (It is something like this: I am here sitting at my desk, occupying space as we say. My occupation has not pushed out any space, for when I move out from here no space comes rushing in to re-occupy the region I have vacated.) 'My' soul or 'my' spirit or 'my' true-self are misconceptions.

The reality is that all that is regarded as 'mine' is nothing other than the one and only 'unpossessable' Total Self, which pours itself out as apparently separate innumerable selves. The existential being is composed of psyche and body, the psycho-physical organism which dies – completely dies. The temporarily embodied universals, which were never born *in time*, never die, for they are eternal. (Since our consciousness is not yet fully awake to the transcendent aspect of Reality, we suffer because of the illusion of separate selfhood.)

Like all the Perfected Holy Ones who had realized Transcendence, Zarathushtra taught figuratively, of necessity. There is no escape from this necessity because Transcendence *is* non-descript. Whatever can be described is confined within the sphere of sense functioning and the logical and imaginative activity of the brain. Transcendence is only suggestible by speech and thought. It was shown earlier (p.26) that 'a described God' can be no other than man apotheosized. The primordial, undifferentiated Creative Energy (name it God, Transcendence, Ahura Mazda, or whatever you please) holds in potentiality within Itself the Totality of all that emerges out of It. When It is stirred into action – Creative Action in Eternity – the indispensable factor for Manifestation (spiritually as Amesha Spentas, Yazads, etc., and materially as space-time, mass-energy, etc. as known by science) is duality: positive-negative, male-female, beginning-ending, life-death, spirit-matter, good-evil, acceptance-rejection, heaven-hell, pleasure-pain – or in Zarathushtra's terminology, *gaya-ajyaiti* etc.

All creatures are discriminatively conscious in terms of duality, and also in terms of multiplicity. Even the Amesha Spentas are regarded as separate from Ahura-Mazda. It had to be so in order that separative self-consciousness might arise and the immense process of involution and evolution, and the development of conscious choice, might take place. Hence the Twin-Spirits, Spenta Mainyu and Angra Mainyu, both of divine origin, emerged out of the Unitary Self of Ahura-Mazda. Ahura, Creative Energy, and Mazda, Divine Wisdom (which is Pure Consciousness) both come into action here. Having created the Twin Spirits, the rest of the universal process is the activity of these Spirits. In the Vendidad (1.1-20), the whole process of creation is presented as Ahura-Mazda creating all that is good, item by item, to each of which Angra Mainyu produces an evil counter-creation. The Upanishads (BU.13.1-21 and CU.1.2.1-8) give a very similar presentation.

In the Judeo-Christian tradition, Lucifer aspires to equality with the Almighty. This inevitably intensifies conflict and gives rise to that inordinate pride which seeks to dominate the other partner. But Lucifer could not reckon with the Absolute Power with which he was dealing. So, from being the brightest one of the angelic host he became lord of the demonic host. Satan is co-ruler of the cosmos (Jesus referred to him as the 'prince of this world'; John, 14.30) but is confined to time and space, which means limitation. Limitation ultimately spells exhaustion. The return journey begins and the Holy Spirit takes charge. The light of heaven brightens and bursts into the transcendent brilliance of the Infinite-Eternal. Space-time, energy-mass, heaven-hell and god-devil (the petty god projected out of man's imperfect mind and the destructive devil born out of and nurtured by man's ignorance, lust and folly) will have finished their allotted tasks and are now transmuted into the Eternal Holy.

Zarathushtra showed the Path out of duality consciousness into Unitary Consciousness. Its name is *asha* – Virtue – and virtuous living is the whole of religious living. It completely subsumes the secular life, the sum-total of our everyday life of politics and economics, upbringing and education, private life and public life, charity and philanthropy, altruism and practical good sense – all of which are somewhat short of unconditional Virtue.

The efficacy of Virtuous living, for promoting human well-being and the fulfilment of the purposes of our existence, is immensely greater than all rituals and ceremonies. This does not mean that rituals and ceremonies should be discarded altogether, for they do have their place in human life and are a real help and comfort for those whose temperament and constitution inclines them that way. But it must be clearly understood that no amount of the external trappings of piety can save a wicked man from the consequences of his evil-doing, despite his private or public prayers or ceremonies. Man is free to act as and when he chooses, if nothing prevents his action; but there is no escape from the result of his act or word or thought. Therefore let every desire or urge, and the response of the intellect to it, be carefully watched before acting. Zarathushtra taught unequivocally (Ys.43.5):

Thou hast ordained through Thy wisdom that all deeds and words shall bear fruit – evil to the evil-doer, good blessings to him who does good, till the end of time.

Judgment lies with God. The vice-gerent of God only announces the Law and advises wisely.

All religions (except Buddhism) invest each man with *an* immortal soul. Whatever is immortal is eternal and infinite, Transcendence itself, the Unitary Whole. If Soul be such, then it cannot be split up into innumerable bits, each of which is appropriated by or attached to a living body, any more than you can slice up space and claim one slice as your own. Just as space as a single whole completely subsumes and interpenetrates countless particular things and persons, so too the One Soul subsumes the whole host of innumerable living persons. This applies to whatever comes under the category of Transcendence, for it belongs to the context of Infinity, Eternity and Immortality. Hence the statement made earlier in this book that each and every manifestation in the universe, be it a thing or a creature, is Transcendence concretized and embodied.

Thus it is absurd to talk of separate, and especially of immortal, souls or spirits. The whole of the One Total Reality is immortal. Even matter is immortal. Take a piece of paper or any convenient lump of matter. Weigh it. Try to annihilate it by, say, burning it. Weigh all the products – the gases, ash, and whatever else is produced. This weight will be the same as the weight of the original sheet of paper, or the material lump, plus the weight of the oxygen used up in the burning. Matter in the shape of paper has changed form – that is all. But the matter that was there at first is still the same amount of matter in a different form, un-annihilatable!

It is even more absurd to hold this postulated separate soul responsible for the body's actions and accord heaven or hell to it. The vast majority of people in the world are vividly conscious of themselves only as bodies and feelings and thoughts; many hold a belief through their cultural conditioning that they have a soul or spirit. Considering the upbringing, education, outlook, ambitions and style of life of the billions of people living today, extremely few have a genuine sensitivity to Transcendence embodied in them. Fewer still are gifted with a natural skill or are fortunate enough to be helped to live in thought and feeling, speech and deed, in accord with their vision of the Divine. Mere implanted beliefs, though presenting exalted concepts couched in high-sounding words, are not that real faith which bears in itself the creative potency of pure Vision which moves one to spontaneous action which is naturally right.

We must relinquish our belief in the soul, the *urvan*, as a separate entity. The concept of *urvan* as a separate entity is our false picture of it. Whatever we are conscious of as possessed of individuality, in the sense of a separate entity, belongs to the context of the perishable. *Urvan*, declared to be immortal, can only be regarded as an all-pervading unitary reality animating all people. Its activity in any person differs from that in any other person in quality and intensity, owing to the influence of the person's own organism and environment. Each and every person is unique in that sense. We may regard *urvan* as that mode of functioning of the Primordial Creative Energy which inclines each person in his own environment to make his particular choice of lifestyle. Will he incline towards Spenta Mainyu or *akem mano*, towards God's Holy Spirit or away from it? In Zarathushtra's day, no one knew that the human body had its age-long evolutionary development from an animal ancestry, and that the brain bears the evidence and carries the influences of this immense past.

The brain, like all our organs, has evolved. It has increased in complexity and capacity for information content over millions of years. Its present structure reflects all the stages through which it has passed. Its oldest part, the brainstem, deals, for example, with heartbeat and respiration, basic functions for bodily existence. Surrounding this is the R-complex which is the source of claim to territory, aggressiveness, social hierarchy and ritual. It has evolved over hundreds of millions of years since the days of our reptilian ancestors and is referred to as our 'crocodile' brain. Surrounding this is the limbic system, or the mammalian brain, evolved tens of millions of years ago in ancestors who were mammals but not yet primates. It is the major source of our moods and emotions, and of our concern and care for the young. Outside this is the cerebral cortex, evolved millions of years ago in our primate ancestors, comprising more than two-thirds of the average human brain mass of about three pounds. The cortex plays the major role in our mental life, its processes distinguishing us from all other animal species and regulating our conscious lives. It is intimately involved with critical analysis, ideas, inspirations, intuitions, reading, writing, mathematics, music, and our whole cultural and spiritual life.

Whereas our 'crocodile' brain may serve as the apparatus for our *akem mano* activity in servitude to Angra Mainyu, and our mammalian brain may help us to advance the more kindly, humane and cooperative aspects of our nature, the cortex is the indispensable instrument for our Spenta Mainyu life of Virtue, *asha*, of pure Intelligence, *vohu-manah*, and of life-energy used in spiritually-directed Creative Action, *khshathra*, in service of the Supreme. The cortex lives in uneasy truce with the R-Complex and the mammalian brain. We must understand that each and every form of energy – deriving from the Primordial Creative Energy, The Origin, which manifests Itself in innumerable forms, whether spiritual, mental or material – must have a suitable apparatus, an efficient instrument, for purposive action and satisfactory result. We see then that the conditions for disharmony lie in our own brain; under sufficiently provocative circumstances open conflict flares up. Our own organism is the battlefield, and also contains the combatants.

Zarathushtra presented this battle as a war to the death against evil. In his very first sermon, he exhorted each individual to consider for himself the teaching about the twin Mainyu before deciding which path to choose: whether to abide by the inspirations of the better (*vahyo*) mind or to succumb to the temptation of the bad (*akem*) mind; whether to follow the good religion of the Truth and live virtuously or be a follower of the Lie and live sinfully. Zarathushtra made it crystal clear that there is judgment after death. It was not Zarathushtra but his followers, centuries after the Prophet's death, who invented descriptions of bliss in Paradise for the righteous and of torment in Hell for the sinful.

So, also, centuries after Zarathushtra's death, the authors of the Pahlavi texts described the Renovation *(frasho-kereti)* and the Final End of all. The angels Airyaman and Atar will melt all the metals in the earth which will flow as a river of glowing molten metal. All mankind will go through this river. The righteous will feel it as warm milk and thereafter live immortally in perfect physical bodies in endless bliss. The wicked will undergo a second death and be wiped out of existence (GBd.34.18-19). Meanwhile, the angelic host will have annihilated all the demons in a last great battle. The river of molten metal will flow down into hell, destroying Angra-Mainyu and burning up every trace of evil in the universe.

Contrasting with the above is a slightly different version. The river of molten metal will purge the wicked souls of all their sins so that they are restored to their pristine purity, and become righteous and worthy of eternal bliss*. The entire creation will become virtuous. Soshoyos, the last of the three Saviours, will perform a ceremony whereby all beings will become immortal. Ohrmazd and his angels fight the last battle and destroy Ahriman and his fiends. Hell is burnt out. Ohrmazd and the heavenly host and all mankind without exception live in eternal bliss thereafter in a renovated world, and the Kingdom of Righteousness is established on earth. The conception presented here that each and every human being will be redeemed, even the worst of sinners, through the last fiery ordeal, seems to be unique to Zarathushtrianism.

Either version, as it stands, is a wonderful example of man's wishful thinking.

What is sadly missing here, as in all the other religions, is the purification and transmutation of the whole Satanic brood into the divine state, and its restoration into the unity of Transcendence, which, in theistic terms, would make God absolutely All in All. All the absurd fantasies produced by man through the ages regarding the end of the

---

*Bd.30.20; Dd.32.12,13; 37.110,111; Mkh.21.10; Dd.14.8; Dk. Vol.5,p.332; Vol.9, p.627.

world and his own ultimate destiny only indicate the immaturity and illogicality of his mind. Someone may say that deep truths are hidden in these symbolic forms. Telling the plain fact in simple language would be more honest and valuable than all this farrago of sheer nonsense, which is, therefore, totally unacceptable.

How can the immaterial soul, *urvan*, be affected by or even contact material conditions and earthly tortures as mentioned earlier (p.60)? And, if *urvan* is declared to be immortal, how can it possibly be annihilated (as one version has it) at the final ordeal? The best we can say of such doctrines is that they are metaphorical, or that they had a pragmatic value in those early days for restraining society from evil-doing by putting the fear of hell into people.

But neither fear nor cruelty nor torture have ever succeeded in making man virtuous. Love and Wisdom alone, *Vohu-Manah* and *Armaiti*, can evoke Virtue. It is necessary to realize that there is no such thing as annihilation – there is only transformation and transmutation. We cannot throw anything out of the cosmos. When a good man becomes a Perfected Holy One and he is capable of being at home not only in the context of the finite and temporal but also of the infinite and eternal, his consciousness has undergone a transmutation. It is only in this 20th century that we have begun to understand the meaning, significance and implications of trans*mutation* as distinct from trans*formation*.

With transmutation, *urvan* – as the discriminator between good and evil, right and wrong, the real and the unreal, and as the chooser of living in accordance with *asha* – is wholly at-oned with *fravashi*. *Fravashi* is the supreme spiritual reality, Ahura-Mazda Himself embodied in the Holy One, who is henceforth unfailingly conscious of Transcendence. The *fravashi* is identical with Spenta Mainyu, and remains absolutely untarnished howsoever a man lives his life.

In the Avesta, there is no statement that Spenta Mainyu or *fravashi* is created; and yet *fravashis* (plural) are spoken of. This plurality we cannot accept. As with *urvan*, *fravashi* belongs to the transcendent context; it is eternally the unitary whole. Spenta Mainyu, permeating every single thing and creature in the universe, is *fravashi*. This permeation of all creation, composed of countless separate particulars, by non-plural Transcendence, without its unitary Wholeness being split up, seems so mysterious to us. We may understand it if we see that it is the individual's incompletely evolved consciousness which splits up the unity like a prism splits up white light into a coloured spectrum. When consciousness has evolved to the full extent possible for the human species, as in the Holy One, the mystery has become the norm for him. He is no longer perplexed; he is at ease, clearly conscious in either context as required.

As stated earlier, this does not mean, however, that the Holy One can present the transcendent context with transparent clarity in terms of the everyday worldly context, that is, in concepts and words, for the descriptive mental images of the worldly context (confined to time, space, matter, measurability, etc.) are absent in the transcendent context. We must bear in mind that the entry into the transcendent consciousness is preceded by the complete calming down and cessation of the discursive thought process and of all psychical turmoil. The peace of God most certainly passes all conceptual-verbal understanding.

None of the founders of the religions of the past or the great mystics were aware of the tremendous influence of the evolutionary process of the human organism, especially of the brain, for enabling a translation into worldly terms of transcendent conscious realization. Nor were they sufficiently cognizant of the fact that the dark, seemingly-solid, impenetrable barrier preventing any easy passage of consciousness in either direction between the Infinite-Eternal-

Immortal and the finite-temporal-mortal became less solid and less impenetrable with the increasing *sure knowledge of the nature of things*, of our everyday experience of the world. This barrier is slowly becoming translucent.

It becomes luminously transparent when a Holy One realizes divine Consciousness and makes the perfect break through into unrestricted Transcendence – like the chick which has broken through the shell, or like the foetus which has emerged as the Divine Babe. Many a babe starts with the potential of divinity within it, but alas!, with extremely rare exceptions, its parents, teachers and friends have not the capacity to evoke and nurture that divinity so that the babe grows into the full-fledged Human, Perfect and Holy, a benediction to his world.

During the last few millennia there have been cracks in the barrier, chinks through which a transcendent ray has enlightened a mortal here, a mortal there. His powerfully-conditioned brain interpreted these spasmodic enlightenments anthropomorphically as gods (super-good and powerful superhumans) and devils or demons (super-evil and powerful inhumans). Every interpretation bears the evidence of humans reading themselves and their worldly life and experience into the nature and lives and actions of their gods and demons. There arose Zarathushtra, Moses, the Upanishadic Holy Ones, the Buddha, Jesus and several others who touched such peaks of Purity, Enlightenment, Compassion, Goodness and Beauty as could possibly be touched in their environment, age and culture. They swept away plurality and affirmed Unity. With the exception of the Buddha and some of the Upanishadic teachers, they presented that Unity anthropomorphically – a Divine Being, Eternal and Immortal.

Such was the culmination they realized. But any being, regarded as a separate entity is not eternal, for every entity derives its separateness from the fact that it comes into being, lives out its life-span and passes away – it is born,

lives and dies. Transcendence is free of all finitude, temporality, mortality and anything and everything that we can
conceive or name. It does not force the universe to grow in
any particular way, like a hot-house plant. It abides by its
own Law – *asha* – which is not compulsive but is gently,
sweetly persuasive, *allowing* the universal process to take
place.

Many faithful devotees of the great religions rigidly
believe that their Teacher was omniscient. He is supposed
to have known everything – the past, present and future;
God, man and the universe; this world and whatever other
worlds there may be; everything without exception was
known or was knowable if he so wished, by him. This is
man's wishful belief, somewhat like a man who, in love
with his own immature picture of love, believes that the
person whom he madly adores is the very incarnation of all
virtue, wisdom, beauty, truth and perfection.

The Holy Ones certainly had perfect understanding of
human nature and insight into Truth. They knew a man
exactly for what he was when they met him, and they knew
the divine nature of Transcendence. They could be consciously in holy relationship with God. And they could
correctly foresee certain things which lay within the pur-
view of their psychological and practical wisdom, *but no
further*, for otherwise they could have predicted in detail all
the developments which have taken place since their day.

They were not infallible in all matters. Some of the
prophecies made by the Buddha and Jesus, for example,
did not transpire, and explanations of natural phenomena,
by the Buddha for instance, were somewhat off the mark.
We revere, adore and worship them none the less. All
mortals, unavoidably make some mistakes. No one can
take full account of the unexpected, the unforeseen and the
unforeseeable in life and nature. In all manifestation there
is the element of elasticity and the unpredictable.

When Zarathushtra spoke of the resurrection and the

frasho-kereti, he had no idea of the absurd picture that
would be put forward many centuries later of the soul
taking up the old buried bones (miraculously enfleshed)
and living immortally on this planet. Apparently this
resurrection is exclusive to Zarathushtrians. So, what
about all the other people who outnumber the Zarathushtrians more than thirty thousand times over? Zarathushtra's
teaching *can* bear a sensible psychological explanation but
unfortunately most people tend to be literal-minded. The
Holy Ones were indeed all-knowing where living virtuously
in accord with Law – *asha, rita, sila, yama,* the command-
ments, etc., both divine and psychological – was concerned.
What good there is in the world today, and real human
flowering, is the fruit of their teaching, for their supreme
concern was human welfare in the true sense, both material
and spiritual.

It should be clearly understood that the sole intention of
critical examination and questioning is *not* to denigrate
any of the great religions or the spiritual Teachers, but to
help us to relinquish all that is unsuitable and unacceptable. Unless we keep in step with all real advances through
the centuries, we will fall short of our fulfilment and duty.

No useful purpose can be served by destructive criticism
or by unnecessarily hurting the feelings of sincere devotees
or causing them mental distress. Our constant and dis-
passionate search for the Truth must always be the driving
force animating our impartial investigations. What the
great Teachers and mystics of the past taught was Truth – as
appropriate for them in their day and age. All reverence
and honour to them. We live today in a scientific age which
has advanced so far as to utterly transform our old concep-
tions of the actual nature of things.

This sharpens our percipience and frees us from super-
stitious beliefs. For example, in ancient times people
believed that thunder and lightning, flood and earthquake,
tempest and volcanic eruption signified the anger and

vengeance of the gods; that mortals who offended them were punished with disease or madness; that comets and eclipses were harbingers of ill-fortune. And they believed that cruel sacrificial rituals involving the death of many animals and of humans were necessary to appease the gods.

In Zarathushtrian Iran there were rites for a person's soul. Cambyses, the Achaemenian King, endowed, in addition to a daily sacrifice of sheep at the tomb of his father*, a monthly sacrifice of a horse for his soul (Arrian, 6.29.7, *Anabasis of Alexander*). Placatory rites in India in olden days involved the cruel and useless slaughter of thousands of innocent animals. Today, only a very small fraction of mankind lives in subjection to such beliefs. Science has also freed man from untenable beliefs concerning the creation of the universe, concerning man, concerning eternal heaven or hell after death, and concerning the 'one and only way' to salvation.

Advances in physiology and psychology have led to clearer understanding of the nature of the human species – with beneficial results in social organization, national and international law, relationships between individuals and nations in everyday life and between mankind and the planet which is his homeland. But in all these spheres, especially the last, man still has a long way to go, because, despite his considerable knowledge of himself as a pyscho-physical organism, he is still ignorant, in depth, of his full human nature. He is still ignorant of his proper place in the scheme of things and his inter-relationship with the Total Reality, and the direction and goal of the evolution of his consciousness. This, coupled with his science and his astonishing technological development has made him a ruthless exploiter of the planet's resources – mineral, plant and animal (including his own species). It is only too well

---

*Cyrus the Great who founded the first Persian Empire after defeating the Medes in 549 BC.

known that he is the most powerful and destructive predator in the world.

How pressingly urgent and significant is the Zarathushtrian teaching concerning the treating of earth, water and fire as pure and sacred! Right use is quite different from insensitive exploitation. We owe our well-being, indeed our very existence, to the elements of Nature. Zarathushtra exhorts us to foster and toil for Earth; she gives us shelter and food. And, through her guardian Spirit (Armaiti), she gives Soul-strength and Renewed Life, perfection and Immortality (Ys.48.5,6)

Science has put extraordinary power into man's hands. Unless there is profound wisdom and all-embracing love, he who wields power almost always misuses it and meets with self-destruction. Worse still, many others are destroyed. If man can wake up in time to the fact that he is fundamentally a religious being who must live as a worthy member of the most highly developed species of the animal kingdom, then he is likely to fulfil his destiny as lord of the world – not as dominator, exploiter and predator, but as protector, nourisher and filial server.

In this century, science has established the inter-convertibility of mass and energy – which has demolished the hitherto rigid wall between the immaterial (energy) and the material (mass). The solid is energy concretized and energy is the solid dematerilized. This dismisses the age-old fixed belief in the absolute separation between spirit and matter, the creator and the created, god and devil – *demon est deus inversus*. The terms 'god' and 'devil' represent polar complementaries of the Primordial Creative Energy in interaction – positive–negative, making–unmaking. When this interaction goes awry, there is what we call 'destruction' or 'accident' in the universal process.

The positive-negative activity builds up and constructs in the 'inanimate' sphere, and gives birth to plants and creatures in the 'animate' sphere. Thus there is a making, a manifesting.

The stability of the manifested depends upon the continuous, balanced cooperation and the proper complementariness of the positive and the negative. In family life, for example, the complementariness of husband and wife, of parents and children.

There comes the stage when the manifested has fulfilled its specific function(s) and the un-making of that particular manifestation must take place. The process of ageing, decay and dissolution sets in, culminating in death – death which is the complete transformation into something new, 'something rich and strange' as Shakespeare said (Tempest, Act 1, Scene 2, Line 399). The same positive-negative brings this about.

The polar complementaries now work in imbalance (not in opposition, not in conflict) with each other, naturally serving the universal law. Struggle, conflict, pain and disease are present when one has not lived in harmony with the Primal Laws of Life – *asha, rita.* But, if one has lived in harmony, dissolution and death can be like the last echo of a sweet song, culminating in the unmaking, the absence of life – Zarathustra's *ajyaiti*.

For a human being, dying can be very wonderful and beautiful if he has dutifully fulfilled his human-ness. Father Time gives sweet release when that supreme moment sounds its irresistible call. And then Eternity enfolds Death (the end of Tme) in its arms and takes him into itself, and the bliss of Peace beyond understanding prevails.

Have you ever, when still and silent, watched sunset glory? Seen the last sun-ray disappearing as the bright gold stallion dips into the sea? Felt the breathless quiet that suffuses you standing on the shore in a twilight lit by a lone star glittering in the west? Listened to the gathering

Gaya (life-promotion) being the making aspect.

darkness till you wake with a start at the love-touch of the Infinite-Eternal? That is Death – the Mainyu which is the divine *ajyaiti* born out of Ahura-Mazda, the One Alone, Lord of *gaya*.

So do not worry over man-made problems regarding the monotheism of Zarathushtrianism, and whether Zarathushtra's teaching is dualistic or not. I myself – ignorant, unwise, misperceiving, imperfect sub-human – I myself am the source, the nourisher and maintainer of all problems. I myself, when purified by *asha*, enlightened by *vohu-manah*, empowered by *khshathra*, am one with *Ahura-Mazda*. And so too can you be, without a shadow of doubt.

6

The Transcendental Vision

The emergence and development of the concept of God, at once the seed and blossom of all theistic religions, is a clear index of man's discovery of the ultimate source and nature of his own self. It epitomizes his Vision of Truth, the Truth which has to flower in him as the fulfilled human creature manifesting perfect humanity. For the theist, the word God is THE WORD, representing the creative source, the maintainer and controller of the whole cosmos. It stands for the Supreme Being, the holiest Sacred, the supreme object of worship, of fervent devotion and deepest veneration. It is the lodestar of his life and the inspiration of his best endeavour.

God does not reveal himself to anyone in the manner in which a person introduces himself to another. God is revealed through a Perfected Holy One, the one of godlike qualities and nature.

Is there any reality, any undeniable fact, denoted by the word God? Or does the word represent some fundamental assumption to serve as a starting point for understanding the world and life, man and his destiny?

If the assumption is incorrect, then all our investigation to discover Truth may prove futile. But if the assumption is not false, then our inquiry will not be a wasted effort. Granting fitness on our part for the quest, it will take us to the very heart of Truth, to Transcendence itself.

We must clearly see that, in this context, inquiry means not only an intellectual exercise but also the dedicated living process of our whole being. Whoso inquires is not merely an external observer; he, as the prime participator, constitutes both the subject and the procedure of the inquiry. He has in fact set out on a journey of self-discovery.

Since this journey is quite unlike a journey in the context of the finite, temporal and mortal, it has no end; it has only a beginning and a proceeding. It has no preconceived or preconceivable goal. He who inquires, seeks No-thing; for Truth is not a thing, not an idea, not an entity of any sort. He has to observe with a completely open mind, free of all beliefs, preconceptions and assumptions. A clean heart, the indispensable basis of purity, *asha*, is necessary, for then the mind is not blind, not biassed, and is capable of seeing the fact as the fact. Passively alert – that is, not looking for something he already knows or desires – and keenly watchful, he awakes to a deeper and deeper Reality in consciousness. In culmination he awakes to the unitary Whole which is identical with the Here-Now, Infinite, Eternal, Immortal.

The entry into deeper and deeper states of consciousness is not like climbing the rungs of a ladder to a greater height, or a movement towards a centre, for a centre is always the limited, finite self. It is an intensification of the awakened state of consciousness. If the voltage of the current passing through a bulb is increased, the light becomes brighter. So too with a man. But if the psycho-physical organism is not sufficiently well prepared to take the full force of the spiritual energy of Transcendence, the result is disastrous.

If he is fit, the intensification culminates, not in a self-centre but in the dimensionless point, the still and silent Here-Now, identical with the Infinite-Eternal. It is the Source of Creation. No brain can describe it, for any description by any mortal organism is confined to the finite, temporal and mortal context.

Such was the Revelation experienced by Zarathushtra at the age of thirty after long years of earnest preparation. In Yasna 43 of his Gatha of Illumination, the *Ushtavaiti*, he discloses with simple devotional fervour how he envisions Ahura-Mazda, his Lord of Life and Wisdom. And he also discloses in this short chapter the secret of the release into the supreme realization, by his affirmation in verse 15: 'Silent meditation is best for the spiritual enlightenment' (see also pp.53 ff. above). To penetrate into the significance and implications of this chapter, we cannot do better than meditate in silence on each of its sixteen verses. In stillness and silence comes the inspiration which each person is capable of receiving according to his mental and spiritual fitness. The genuine experience of Revelation is overwhelmingly impressive and absolutely convincing. It is characterized by an all-inclusive wholeness and an immediacy in which nothing comes between the Holy One and Transcendence.

In the Pahlavi account given by the 9th century writer Zadspram, Zarathushtra's experience is briefly described. It is likely that Zadspram, a more liberal minded man than his elder brother Manuschihr, may have experienced illumination on rare occasions. Possibly based on these he attempted to describe Zarathushtra's experience. Although the Holy One's transcendent realization is beyond all description, Zadspram's description can be suggestive. In the Pahlavi work (Zadspram, 20,21) it is said that Zarathushtra went alone at dawn to fetch water from the middle of a river for a *haoma* ceremony (to celebrate a spring festival with all those present). On returning to the bank he saw a shining Being, Vohu Manah, who led him to Ahura Mazda and five other shining Beings. From these Seven he received his Revelation.

It is not easy to visualize what could have happened. But see! The time is the early dawn. The cleansing water of the cool stream, the lovely colouring of the sky and the beauty of distant peaks changing swiftly from blue to rose pink and bright gold as the sun climbs above the horizon; all have a quietening and uplifting spiritual influence. There is a curiously peaceful exhilaration for the disciplined mind. Zarathushtra's feet hardly seem to touch the earth as he walks on. An extraordinary calm pervades everything and without any expectancy on his part there is an intense awareness that the Presence is here, felt, 'seen'. And so the fervent devotee's longing of the years finds fulfilment in meeting the forms shaped by the conditioning of the psyche since childhood. Thus it is that Zarathushtra 'sees' Ahura-Mazda and the Holy Immortals, 'converses' with them, and receives the Revelation and the Divine Mandate to teach the Good Religion, salve humanity, and prepare the world for the Renovation at the end of Time.

Probably, Zarathushtra actually entered the silent meditative state of the Supreme Communion, consciously realized the Infinite-Eternal, and arose as the divinely-appointed Teacher. It could all have happened in the instantaneous immediacy of the Here-Now as he stepped onto the river bank to officiate as the celebrant of the ceremony; or as he sat cross-legged before the sacred fire.

Did those present realize that Zarathushtra the priest was now the sanctified Prophet? Perhaps they did sense a spiritual power in that transformed atmosphere. Some may even have glimpsed a transfigured Being. Amongst the founders of the great religions, Zarathushtra is the one example of a fully qualified priest – a *Zaotar* as he calls himself in Yasna 33.6, and a *Manthran* in Yasna 32.13 – who was also a Prophet (*Ratu* in Yasna 31.2.)

There were further occasions of Supreme Communion in which Ahura-Mazda summons Zarathushtra to his service. The Prophet implicitly obeys his God. He affirms in Yasna 44.11:

For this (service) *was I set apart as Thine.*

And in Yasna 28.4 we have his self-dedication:

As long as I have will and strength, so long will I exhort men to strive for asha.

The ancient Indo-Iranians worshipped cult gods such as Fire and Water, and also nature gods such as Sun, Moon, Sky, Earth, etc. There were two gods of Wind: Vata, the wind that blows and brings rain-bearing clouds; and Vayu, the breath of life for the Iranians, the soul of the gods for the Indians. The concepts of the Holy Spirit (Spenta Mainyu) and the spirit in man *(fravashi)* may have grown out of this concept of Vayu. The Indo-Iranians believed that the universal process was governed by Law which was immutable. The gods themselves obeyed it. It operated not only in natural phenomena but also in the conduct of gods and men. The Rigvedic Varuna was the *moral* governor of the universe, ruled by Rita. The Gathic Ahura-Mazda was the very embodiment of *asha*, the undeviating moral law of Truth, Order and Justice. The righteous ones, men or gods, upheld *asha*. They were *ashavants*. Their opposites, wicked men and demons, were *dregvants* for they served the Evil Principle, the *druj*, the Lie, Sin.

The Indo-Iranians attached special sacredness to man's spoken word. Varuna was the lord of the solemn oath, Mithra (Vedic Mitra) of the compact or agreement between man and man. In the Avesta, Varuna is known only by his other name, Apam Napat, child of the waters, the moisture in the rain-clouds. Apam Napat is the lightning form of fire *(agni)*. In the Rigveda (7.49.3) the *asura* (Lord) Varuna moves in the midst of the waters indispensable for all that is living.

In the upholding of justice, the ordeal by water (Varuna's element) or by fire (Mithra's element) decided guilt if the accused died, or innocence if he survived. Since the ordeal had such a serious result, the king or the leader of the tribe had to decide whether an ordeal was necessary. Therefore the ruler, who was the ultimate justiciar, had to be supremely wise. Thus arose the concept of Ahura-Mazda, the Lord of Wisdom, the greatest of the three Ahuras – Mithra and Apam Napat being the other two. And since a lord had power only if he was alive, any Ahura had to be a living God, Lord of Life.

Of these three Ahuras of the Indo-Iranians, guardians of *asha*, Mazda had been worshipped as the greatest. Zarathushtra made a revolutionary change (probably after one of his silent meditative states in Supreme Communion) by declaring that Ahura-Mazda was the one and only Un-created God, self-existent, eternal, the sole Creator of all the beneficent divinities and of everything that is good in the universe, all-wise, absolutely just and good.

Zarathushtra sings of his Vision of Ahura-Mazda as He whose Light set alight all the lights of the empyrean; as He who through His Wisdom created *asha* through which He upholds His Sovereign Mind (Ys.31.7); as He who is the Ancient of Ancients and also the Youngest of the Young, Eternal, the Father of Vohu Manah (Ys.31.8; 45.4), the Judge Supreme of the deeds of all who live (Ys.31.8). His is Armaiti, she of good works, devotion and good faith (Ys.31.9; 45.4). He is the Maker of bodies, souls and mental powers, the One who breathed life-breath into mortal bodies, gave abilities to act and teachings to guide (Ys.31.11). He is the Creator of all things (Ys.44.7). He is most worthy to be invoked, the Holy Judge of actions, Lord of Truth (Ys.46.9), Mighty, Holy (Ys.43.4)

To the above we must add what is said in Chapter Three (p.27) regarding Ahura-Mazda's iteration of his Divine Names, in answer to Zarathushtra's request. The Lord says: 'My first name is *ahmi*, I AM (the Living One); the Gatherer (or, the Shepherd); the Omnipresent; Supreme Righteousness; the whole Good Creation of the seed of *asha* (distinguishing it from the marring of the Creation by Angra Mainyu); Knowledge and its Possessor; Wisdom and its Master; the Omniscient One; Joy of Life (or Spiritual Prosperity); the Bestower of fruitfulness; Lord of Life; Almighty and Undefeated (Omnipotent); Universal Friend; Just Accountant; All-seeing; Healer; Creator.' And finally –

reiterating the first name – 'I am that Mazda, I AM.' Who-
ever the composer of the Ahura-Mazda Yasht was, the
pronouncement of the Names is an expression of Zarathushtra's own personal realization in one of his profoundest
Communions. This he divulged to his foremost disciple,
the 'son' of the prophet, who in his turn passed it on to his
'son', and so on down to the writer of the Yasht. All this,
together with his own sayings in the Gathas and the words
of Ahura-Mazda regarding his 'abode' where dwell the
Holy Immortals (p.27 above), represents Zarathushtra's
TRANSCENDENTAL VISION OF AHURA-MAZDA.

Thus far did Zarathushtra go in his pronouncements. It
was not possible in those ancient days to go deeper. Nevertheless, Zarathushtra freed his people from the obscuration
caused by the worship of many gods. Zarathushtra's God is
a Unitary Being. This took men a long step closer to unitary
Wholeness. Ahura-Mazda is Wisdom/Eternal Life – in
modern terms, Pure Consciousness/Creative Energy. But
such terms could not be used in those old days, for the
advancement of verbal expression depends upon the
advance in the knowledge of the nature of things, that is,
upon the developments in all sciences.

Science is the knowledge of the universe (including man)
which is the expression in the context of the finite and
mortal of the Infinite-Eternal, of God as Transcendence. A
man's signature can tell us something of the man. The
Creation is God's signature. And what a wonderfully
revealing signature it is – if only we read it correctly. When
we read it correctly, we are cleansed of Untruth, of the Lie.
Science is the servitor of Truth. It is only as far as verbal
expression is concerned that Zarathushtra could go no
further. As far as the actual Communion was concerned, he
realized the supreme state which man can possibly realize.

Thus Zarathushtra completed his journey of self-
discovery. By realizing the Supreme communion he
uncovered his integral unity with Ahura-Mazda. He

touched the peak of an ascending arc of spiritual vision, moving up from a medley of gods and godlings to a Single, Supreme Being, the transcendent counterpart of the all-powerful earthly overlord of any tribal society of those days. Since the context of Transcendence is the Infinite and Eternal, everything concerning this Supreme Being – his Wisdom, Purity, Power, Justice, Perfection, etc. – had to be Absolute.

The Perfected Holy One of any historical period has to couch his teachings in forms suitable to the times, the receptivity of the people, and their pressing spiritual and psychological needs. The transcendent context of the Infinite-Eternal negates the limited everyday context of the finite and mortal (see p. 19). There is no human language to express the Transcendent. But since the transcendent context does not destroy but fully subsumes and interpenetrates the mortal context, each Teacher conveyed the transcendental spiritual values or characteristics by using the ordinary terms of our human values and raising them to the ultimate degree to suggest Divine Values.

But now difficulties arise. We would say quite logically that absolute or transcendent love cannot include hurting or destroying any creature or plant or person. Hence it is interesting to consider Zarathushtra's words in Yasna 31.18:

Let none of you give ear to the words and teachings of the follower of the Druj (Untruth), for he will give over the house, the town, the province and the country to destruction and death. So, resist him with weapons.

To soften the ferocity of the last sentence some scholars have resorted to the use of mollifying qualifications: 'Resist with (spiritual) weapons'; 'Resist with the dart (of your spirit)'; 'Resist with a blow'; 'You should triumph with the weapon (viz. religion).' Martin Haug, in his *Essays on the Religion of the Parsis* (p. 152), frankly translated this as 'Kill him with the sword.' This might well express Zarathushtra's honest sentiment.

Zarathushtra well knew the evil and destructiveness of raiding marauders. The agriculturists of the settlements had to be protected by the warrior caste – and a warrior who uses no weapons is not an .efficient protector. Inflexibly opposed to all evil – cruelty, wickedness, injustice, spoliation – Zarathushtra, the champion of Ahura-Mazda, worked indefatigably for the *destruction* of evil, which involved the elimination of the evil-doer. Time and again the Holy Ones have suffered defeat at the hands of circumstance. Most people are unaware that the perfect thing happens only in the ripeness of circumstance.

We gather from the Pahlavi books what Zarathushtra taught about Creation. Ahura-Mazda created first the universe in an immaterial, spiritual state, called *menog*, which was followed by its materialization, the *getig* state. This was considered a better state than the spiritual state, for solid and sentient form was regarded as an added good. Creating these two states was the *Bundahishn*, the Creative Act. Now came trouble. The spiritual, being immaterial, was invulnerable. But the material could be spoilt. Angra Mainyu attacked at once, marring the perfection of sky, water, earth, plant, animal, man, and fire. The Holy Immortals came to the rescue. They dealt with the spheres that came under their jurisdiction, and produced much good for the future for man and the universe. However, whereas Ahura Mazda had brought forth life and growth and happiness through his Holy Spirit, Angra Mainyu introduced decay and death and misery into the world.

How and whence did the Evil Spirit come upon the scene? Zarathushtra suddently introduces him on the world stage in his first sermon without a word of explanation of how or whence. If there was any teaching by Zarathushtra in this connection, Macedonian and Arab, Turk and Mongol effectively destroyed it with the burning of the books and massacres of the priests in whose memory all this knowledge was locked. Notwithstanding every tragedy, there is enough treasure left in the Gathas to show us that the Prophet of Ancient Iran started a new chapter, of profound consequence to mankind, in the Book of Life.

First, on the material side, Zarathushtra exalted care of the Earth, Armaiti, our Mother to whom reverence was due. (Was Zarathushtra then the earliest ecologist and environmentalist of the Indo-European peoples?) He praised agriculture. He exhorted his people to base a peace-loving society on subsistence agriculture – which has been one of the main factors for the promotion of our cultural developments, of just and humane relationships between man and man, between man and animal, and of decent and intelligent civilized living. If we cannot love and revere our own Mother, we are likely to remain robbers and murderers, as were the inhuman, marauding raiders about whose destructiveness Zarathushtra wailed unto his God (Ys.46.1,2;48.11;49.1,2;50.1,3).

Next, in the spiritual sphere, Zarathushtra was the first to present the concept of a sole, supreme, Divine Being, a transcendent Creator God, an absolutely Just Ruler of His Universe in accord with the Law as ordained by Him, the Law of Righteousness, Truth and Order. Unlike the gods of some of the pantheons of the human race, Ahura Mazda never deviated from the strictest observance of His own Law.

Zarathushtra's exalted and sublime conception seems, however, to lack much emphasis upon Love and Mercy. This is not surprising; for if Righteousness and Justice are to be absolute, Justice tempered with Mercy, or Unrighteousness condoned with Forgiveness, would spell the blunting of absoluteness. This aspect of Divinity – Love, Compassion, Forgiveness, Mercy – was to find its blossoming some ten to fifteen centuries after Zarathushtra.

He was also the first to promulgate doctrines which, in course of time, became articles of faith in other religions – the immortality of the soul and its judgement by God after death, heaven and hell, bodily resurrection, final judgement and second death or eternal bliss.

In Zarathushtra's life and teaching, prayer played a very important part for invoking God, the Holy Immortals and the beneficent divinities whose powers and spiritual energies could be evoked and utilized for purifying and healing the psyche. Praying in front of the sacred fire induced profound enstasy in Zarathushtra. It induced the pure, silent, meditative state of at-one-ment with Ahura Mazda in which the Revelation of Truth took place and the ecstatic utterances of the Gathas emerged. In Yasna 33.4 he says something quite extraordinary about the power of prayer:

Therefore, O Mazda, I will pray away (exorcise?) *doubt and ill intent from Thy worshippers, perversity of mind from the Self-Reliant, hostility of the nearest kin from the Co-worker, slander from the Friend, and the wicked herdsman* (the False Teacher) *from the land* (the 'Pasture of the cow').*

Such is Zarathushtra's psychic power, the 'white magic', *khshathra*, of the pure magus.

Zarathushtrianism prescribes numerous rituals for various occasions. Some of the more important were: the daily priestly act of worship, the *yasna*; the *naojot*, the initiation ceremony of full admission into the Zarathushtrian faith, when the young boy or girl is invested by the priest with the consecrated shirt, the *sudra*, and the sacred girdle, the *kusti*; the betrothal and wedding ceremonies and ceremonies associated with death. Then there are the many short ritualistic observances for the daily maintenance of bodily and mental purity.

Zarathushtrianism holds an exalted view of marriage and family. Ahura Mazda says to Zarathushtra (Vd. 4.47):

---

*The Self-Reliant, Co-worker and Friend were the three grades of the disciples of Zarathushtra, the Self-Reliant being the highest.

Spitama Zarathushtra! He who has a wife is superior to him who has not; he who has a family and children is superior to him who has not.

Zarathushtra asks (Vd.3.2):

O Creator of the world! Which is the second place on earth that feels happy?

Ahura Mazda answers:

That place over which a holy man builds a house with fire, cattle, wife, children and good followers.

Unmarried maidens pray thus for a husband (Yt.15.40):

*Grant us this boon, that we may obtain young and handsome husbands who will treat us with kindness all our life, and give us offspring – wise, learned, ready-tongued husbands.**

And each one prays for children (Ys.62.4,5):

Give me, O Atar! (the angel of Fire) strong, steady, firm-footed, watchful, wakeful, energetic offspring, helpful, supporting, virtuous, intelligent, ruling and presiding over meetings and assemblies, possessing power and influence, clever, delivering men from misery and woe, strong and brave as a hero, offspring that may promote my family and house, town, province and country, and its religion.

In the *Vahishta-Ishti* Gatha, these words are addressed to Pouruchisti, the devoted daughter of Zarathushtra (Ys.53.3):

May Ahura Mazda give thee as a husband the man who is the companion of Asha, Vohu Manah and Mazda. So greet him with whole-hearted trust, and pour upon him the nectar of thy holiest devotion.

In verse 5, Zarathustra earnestly advises all brides and

*At the age of fifteen and over, young men and women were regarded as fit to marry.

bridegrooms to love each other through *asha*, for it is only that kind of mutual love which brings rich fulfilment.

It was considered a meritorious act for a Zarathushtrian to help one of the faithful to marry (Vd.4.44):

When men of the same faith come here seeking a field, or a wife, or wisdom, then you should help them to obtain a field, or a wife, and you should recite the sacred texts to them.

Zarathushtrianism has no use for asceticism and is opposed to celibacy and the unmarried state. During the 3rd century AD., Mani, an Iranian of noble blood, propagated an eclectic religion, composed of various tenets chosen from Zarathushtrianism, Christianity, Buddhism and Syrian Gnosticism. He declared that the body (matter) was the root of evil. Salvation could be won only by poverty, fasting, celibacy and complete self-mortification, all of which are entirely foreign to the spirit of Zarathushtrianism. Moreover, he presented a dualistic theology of conflict between light and darkness, Ohrmazd and Ahriman. After some preliminary success during the reigns of Shabuhr I (AD 240-72) and Hormizd I (AD 272-3), his trial and execution, engineered by Kirder, the most powerful cleric of the day, took place in the reign of Vahram I (AD 273-6).

Some two-and-a-half centuries later, there arose another self-appointed prophet, Mazdak, whose doctrines, like those of Mani, were pessimistic. But he upheld tolerance, kindliness and brotherhood, carrying the last to the extent of preaching the holding of property in common and, as some said, of women too. There was also a tendency towards asceticism. Near the end of Kavad's reign, the king allowed his third son, Khosrow, to arrange a banquet, in AD 528, in honour of Mazdak; but unfortunately for this minor prophet, he and many of his followers were slaughtered there. Treachery and murder have left dark stains on the history of the religions of the world.

Zarathushtra was a man of action. According to Zarathushtrian views, deeds were more important than speech
and thought. The true Zarathushtrian tries to live his life
virtuously, by *asha*. He may even realize sainthood thereby.
But he seeks more assiduously to express this in daily life in
society, in the everyday world, which necessitates service to
the people and the state through his special skills, philanthropy and charity. He may also be required to act to
prevent others from wrong-doing – which can raise difficult problems. Bearing in mind Zarathushtra's own
admonition to his listeners (Ys.30.2) to consider carefully
what he said to them, and then 'decide, each man for
himself' what course of action he should follow, one
wonders what sort of social order might prevail if each
member of society took it upon himself to prevent his
'erring' neighbours' activities.

Many people shy away from religion because they feel
that to be religious means to be solemn, to shun the legi-
timate joys of everyday life, to spend one's life praying and
fasting; in short, to be miserable.

Nothing could be further from the truth. Religious living
simply means living the daily secular life virtuously. It can
well include prayer and worship, for these are spontaneous
expressions of man's tenderly growing awareness of Transcendence, and of the fact that he is primarily a religious
being and only secondarily everything else. Zarathushtra
as a man of action and as a Prophet of God was a very
practical man with sound psychological insight. He well
knew that men will of course run away from a misery agent,
but incline favourably towards a happiness bringer. So he
affirmed that not only God but also this physical world is
good. Thus one of the outstanding features of Zarathushtrian religion is its joyousness.

Zarathushtra says:

O far-seeing Lord of Life, reveal to me for my joy your priceless gifts of Khshathra which are the blessings of Vohu Manah. (Ys.33.13)

Tell me truly, O Ahura . . . for whom didst Thou fashion this joy-giving Earth? (Ys.44.6)

Tell me truly, O Ahura. How may I walk in beatific joy with you, in full companionship? (Ys.44.17)

Of this (Holy) *Spirit, Thou art indeed the Holy Father; Thou didst create this Earth for our joy.* (Ys.47.3)

Zarathushtra laid two binding obligations on his followers. One was the five short daily prayers – morning, noon, afternoon, evening and night – in praise of Ahura Mazda and execration of Angra Mainyu. The other was to celebrate seven high feasts every year, one to Ahura Mazda at the spring equinox, and the other six to the six Amesha Spentas – at mid-spring, mid-summer, mid-winter and the feast days of Bringing in the Corn, of Homecoming of the Herds from Pasture, and of the *fravashis* on the last night of the year before the spring equinox.

Celebrations began with religious services early in the day; later on there were joyful gatherings with communal feasts. All the people, high and low, rich and poor, met and mingled freely, exchanging friendly greetings and strengthening their bonds as members of the Zarathushtrian faith. Zarathushtrianism is a life-affirming faith and it is a Zarathushtrian characteristic to take full advantage of any opportunity for merry-making.

Two thousand years after the great Prophet of Ancient Iran spoke and legislated, the sun of joy was eclipsed by the Arab conquest. A dark age began for the Zarathushtrians of Iran, growing darker and darker with invasion after invasion*.

*The epic story is well told by Mary Boyce, Professor Emeritus of Iranian studies, University of London, in her recent book, *Zoroastrians: Their Religious Beliefs and Practices*. (See Bibliography.)

The Zarathushtrians drank their cup of sorrow to the dregs. Century after century, with singular courage, endurance, patience, fortitude and unwavering loyalty to their religion, they suffered insults, humiliation, tortures, poverty and degradation inflicted upon them by Muslim officials and rulers. To this day the Iranian Zarathushtrians know the meaning of oppression and suffering. But, though the joy of life may have become heavily clouded for them, the sun of Zarathushtra's teaching still shines in their souls, a quenchless light.

In those Ahrimanic times, a band of Zarathushtrian men, women and children from Sanjan in south-west Khorasan, moved south to Hormuzd on the Persian Gulf, secured a ship and sailed away eastwards. Nineteen years were spent on the island of Div before they finally landed on the coast of Gujrat in AD 936. Those immigrants into India are the people now called Parsis. Over a period of a thousand years, the terms 'Parsi' and 'Zarathushtrian' have become practically synonymous. Humane India, tradition-ally a mother to all people, especially to those in distress, protected this refugee band in her sheltering arms. Their story, wherever they have settled abroad has been one of humble beginnings, of loyal adherence to their religion and traditions and of fidelity to the ruling powers in the lands of their settlement, all of which has led them through a millennium of success and prosperity, and has won for them universal respect for character and achievements in all spheres. They have done well and have never failed as a community to benefit those lands of their settlement. But in this century some awkward problems, needing skilful treatment, have arisen for the community and the religion.

7
The Way Forward

It may well be that, in the early days of the human race, dreams about the dead gave rise to the belief in the survival of an immortal spirit after bodily death. In course of time, spirits were associated with everything in the world of Nature. As Nature was beneficent and kindly or harmful and cruel, so these spirits were accordingly regarded as good or evil. By analogy with their own tribal chiefs, the spirits must have had their own rulers, the gods, who were regarded with awe. So too were the shamans and priests who mediated between the gods and men.

Systems of ceremonial worship came into being expressing man's gratitude and submission to the beneficent divinities and seeking their favours and protection. Placatory rites with offerings – mainly the senseless slaughter of animals and even humans – were devised to ward off the anger and vengeance of the demons, or appease the spirits. Blood-sacrifices were a common sanguinary feature of the religious practices of ignorant and fearful primitives.

On the happy side, man, endowed with a sense of wonder, was not unresponsive to the marvel and beauty of Nature and of the living process of the whole world. Pain and fear were not the only features in life. There was also joy – exultant pleasure in his own physical prowess and skill, delirious delight with his (or her) mate, and the protective possessiveness of proud parenthood. There were deep sensuous satisfactions – dawns and sunsets, the trickling of cool water, bird calls and songs, fragrance of flower and field, star-shine, pleasant food and the friendly company of man and animal. True, there were difficulties and sorrows to counter all these joys. But when the joy of life courses through the blood, youthful energy triumphs over many a difficulty. Primitives enjoyed a free *participation mystique* with nature, denied to most moderns.

Scores of millennia rolled on. As man's sensitivities grew, he came to realize that there was THAT which lay altogether beyond him, except when a lightning flash from THAT rendered him incapable of denying Transcendence.

Such flashes struck him when he was not self-preoccupied, when he was silent and still, not struggling to find his god or himself, and decidedly not striving to assert himself against Nature or his neighbour. That magical flash was the starting point of the enlightening – the awakening of his consciousness from its aeonian slumber. It showed him the whole Way to his full awakening to the Transcendence embodied in him.

That whole Way is immeasurable; yet it is entirely contained in the spot on which man stands; such is the mystery of the transmutation of consciousness from the mode of finitude into that of Infinity. And the time it takes to traverse that Way is also immeasurable. It is instantaneous, for that is the magic of Eternity. You can never 'know' any true magic. You can only *do* it, Here-Now. Simple, but incredibly difficult; perplexing and elusive.

Nature's task was to evolve the human organism out of the primate. Man's responsibility is to emerge out of the prison-house of isolative self-consciousness into the freedom of unitarily Whole Consciousness. But the duration of the one process is entirely different from that of the other, because the former, concerned with matter, takes place in the context of the finite and temporal, whereas the latter, concerned with spirit, lies in the context of the Infinite and Eternal.

Zarathushtra was probably the earliest of the Holy Ones who realized this responsibility. He had to communicate it in the circumscribed forms of the speech and thought of his day. So he brought the several beneficent gods or powers of the old Indo-Iranians under the suzerainty of the One Supreme God, Ahura Mazda, who, with his six Amesha Spentas are:

... of one mind, one voice, one act ... Of them, one beholds the soul of the other, thinking upon good thoughts, good words good deeds ... they who are the creators, fashioners, makers, observers and guardians of the creation of Ahura Mazda. (Yt. 19.16-18)

This was the first great step towards unitary Wholeness; but it was confined to the context of the Good. Zarathushtra, however, knew all too well from experience that cruelty, injustice and wickedness existed, utterly opposed in nature to the Good. He regarded it as existing co-terminously with the Good, throughout all time.

Angra Mainyu, uncreated, ignorant and malign, is the ruling spirit of this evil, and he is the unitarily whole representative of Evil. But to have two unitarily whole spirits is illogical. Furthermore Zarathushtra presents the two Spirits as Twins. Therefore the Good Spirit and the Evil Spirit must have come into being at the same time. Hence the later Avesta presented Ohrmazd as the 'One who ever was, is and will ever be,' and Angra Mainyu as the 'One who was, is, but will not ever be.' Whereas the Good Spirit is Eternal, the evil spirit is only temporal.

Three thousand five hundred years ago it was impossible not to postulate a single Lord of Evil as the master of all evil in the world. Zarathushtra clearly saw the undeniable fact of the existence of evil. He stated the fact in the only possible way which fitted the climate of belief in his day.

His doctrine of the Twin Mainyu, as propounded by him, has given rise to a troublesome question: Is Zarathushtrianism a dualistic religion?

The opponents of the religion present it as a dualism. So it would be, if Angra Mainyu is not merely co-terminous with Ahura Mazda and his Holy Spirit but is actually eternal and hence indestructible. But according to the later Zarathushtrian teaching expounding Zarathushtra's baldly announced doctrine of Renovation after the end of time, Angra Mainyu – and his brood, and hell, and the wicked souls – will be utterly destroyed (see page 72 above). Ahura Mazda thus remains absolute God without any equal. Zarathushtrianism cannot, therefore, be regarded basically as a dualism.

Time is subsumed by Eternity. At the end of time – that is, when time dies – there is only Eternity, unitary Wholeness alone, in which dualism is not. In the transcendent Consciousness of unitary Wholeness, no question propounded by us has the slightest meaning. All questions vanish there, like Angra Mainyu at the end of time. Wisdom lies in abolishing this question of dualism. Then there is the beatitude of ineffable peace, wherein nothing is done or stirred up, and yet everything happens. Such is the Khshathra Vairya, the Desirable Kingdom, and the Might, Majesty and Creative Power of Ahura Mazda.

It was pointed out earlier (p.16) that we are separatively and isolatively self-conscious. Therefore we are mainly self-concerned and self-centred, except where our own family or social group is involved. Our interests, ambitions and desires are self-oriented. Since these are different for each person or each small group, the situation is always one of competition or conflict. The nations of the world, great or small, live in fear and suspicion of each other. Their inter-relationships are bound by strict, jealously-guarded conditions, laid down by each side. Armaments pile up.

As on the large scale, so on the small, personal scale. Because of our ignorance, fears, hates, greeds, desires, likes and dislikes, we are often in a state of disharmony within ourselves and with our neighbours. All the causes of disease and disharmony, failure and sorrow, lie partly outside us and mainly within us. We are still sub-human, growing slowly towards healthy and happy human-ness. But if we, the individuals comprising the human race become sane, healthy and skilful – and it is always the character and abilities of individuals which determine the course of history for better or worse – we may avoid destruction.

Religious living is that way of living which will inevitably make and keep us sane, skilful and healthy (whole, holy), and lead us to life and liberty, to *vahishtem ahum*, the Best Life. Zarathushtra's genius embodied the whole way of salvation in one word: *asha* (virtue).

All the great religions are agreed on this point. VIRTUE is a magical power which can completely purify and heal the psyche and rightly solve all the problems with which the whole human race is beset. It is a power compounded of humility, harmlessness, and selflessness; of purity, righteousness and truth; of compassion, wisdom and goodness; of love; of beauty. Virtue is the Song of the Spirit.

Zarathushtra summed up the practice of Virtue in the simplest and most practical way: *humata, hukhta, hvarshta* – good thoughts, good words, good deeds.

This necessitates constant watchfulness. Calmly observe all thoughts and feelings, words and actions. Notice how they arise, proceed and pass away. They all belong to the realm of the finite and mortal. Note whether they are good or evil, sensible or stupid; but do not pass any judgement on yourself because of them. Approval will increase self-esteem and conceit; condemnation will produce guilt; both are obstructions to healthy growth.

Genuine virtue is not Pharisaical. Its active presence in one is not noticeable by oneself, but is visible like a beacon light to others. When the brain is unaware of one's own virtue, then Virtue is the substance of one's psyche.

Consciousness, freed of the dead weight of selfness, shines then with the light of Transcendence, so that all thought and feeling, word and action is pure and holy. Unitarily Whole Consciousness signifies that Ahura Mazda (Transcendence) is functioning freely through you. When *akem mainyu*, the evil spirit, afflicts consciousness, then thought and feeling, speech and action are expressions of Angra Mainyu's triumph. When Ahura Mazda, in his aspect of *asha vahishta*, highest virtue, functions freely through one's being, consciousness is at home in the Infinite-Eternal and one experiences *haurvatat* (supreme well-being) and *ameretat* (immortality) here-now, whilst bodily alive.

The usual approach to religious living is a self-centred one. I live religiously in order to insure my spiritual security – a safe place in heaven for me after my death, for I dread the torments of hell! A radical change is required. I have to realize that there is nothing whatsoever for me the existential being, for there is no such thing as a self which is a permanent identifiable entity. I, whilst I am alive, think and speak and act. The One Total Reality, as well as I during my lifetime, reap the consequences of all that I think, speak and do. Throughout my life I bear a serious and constant responsibility to the Totality, to Transcendence, to God the unitary Whole. I have to grow out of separative self-consciousness into unitarily Whole Consciousness. I must cease to live and work exclusively for myself and my little circle, and live and work for all humanity. The self-centred consciousness and activity must be transformed into the Holistic, imbued by *asha* which is the Law for the whole universal process and for our personal lives.

The great Teachers were profoundly concerned with our happiness and well-being, and with showing us how to transform our isolative I-consciousness, which is the sorrow-bringing and division-making consciousness, into the all-inclusive Us-consciousness, which is unitive, blissful and universal. They were the true 'Socialists', transcendentally so. Their Socialism has nothing in common with all the pseudo-socialisms in the world, which are only partisan and self-concerned. True Socialism is impossible without an us-consciousness in the full sense, where no one is separate from, but is in full relationship with all humanity.

Such consciousness is not a case of having a vision but of actually *being* the VISION, not merely seeing a distant light but *being* the LIGHT itself. When all illusory beliefs, ideas and convictions are out, you ARE the TRUTH.

When the mortal self relinquishes and dies to all selfness, Ahura Mazda is here. Remember what Porphyry said (*Life of Pythagoras*, 41): 'Ahura Mazda's Body is Light and his Spirit is Truth.' That Light and Truth subsumes and suffuses you, and is YOU, the Perfected Holy One.

Beliefs, doctrines, dogmas, convictions and certainties – these clip the wings of the spirit as you attempt the uncharted flight in the trackless open towards the Unknown Transcendence. Having studied, understood, loved and lived in harmony with the Avesta (or Gita, or Bible, or Veda, or Dhammapada, or any other 'finger of light' pointing to your destination), cling to none of them. Give away, as a Love-gift, everything you have and everything you are to anyone and everyone you meet. Burn away in the sacred fire of self-sacrifice, knowing that sacrifice has only one true meaning, making sacred. This fire needs no sandalwood or incense. Transcendence finds no sacrifice more acceptable than the sacrifice of its own divine Self imprisoned in you. Sacrificing thus, 'you' the ephemeral appearance of temporal reality are released into the Immortal Reality of the Infinite-Eternal. YOU become one with the absolute I AM.

Never forget that 'you' and 'your' God (flung out of your brain) are substanceless nothings! That all your huffing and puffing to tread the path are vain imaginings – for your

body is the Path, and Consciousness is the Traveller –
leaving you exhausted, ready for death, like the spent leaf
on the earth awaiting winter's blast! That the truly religious
life is no other than dying ecstatically out of decaying Time
into ever newborn and life-abounding Eternity.

Wake up, brother, and die to all selfness, and you will
hear the honey-sweet voice of God singing softly in the
unknown divine language, which you will understand im-
mediately without labouring to learn it, telling you: 'Well
done, Beloved Child, well done! How I have longed
through the twilit glooms of age-long Time for this
Supreme Bliss of your Home-Coming. Come, Beloved,
come! For you are my very own Self returned to Eternal
Being, and restored to perfect Holiness free of any stain of
Ill. You have also purified and transmuted Ahriman and his
host. Behold them here in my very Being, redeemed, and
changed into their Original Light! O my Champion! Thou
art the noble, heroic son of good Mother Earth, a true
Human.'

Hark! Saoshyant of the seed of Zarathushtra stands by
and calls:

Awake! And hear!

Build the Desirable Dominion on God's Earth!

Bibliography

The collected sacred texts of Zarathushtrianism, the Avesta, consist of many compositions spread over an immense time-span of nearly twenty centuries. The earliest, attributed to Zarathushtra himself, are the seventeen surviving Gathas (hymns or poems or psalms) in an ancient, eastern Iranian language, Gathic Avestan (close in its forms to Indian Rigvedic). These Gathas, transmitted orally for many centuries, are the only examples of Gathic Avestan literature. They contain many words of unknown or uncertain meaning; the grammar and syntax are very complex. Hence, they are extraordinarily difficult to translate, and there are wide differences is all translations into modern languages.

In the Sasanian Empire (c. AD 224-651), a canon of all Avestan texts was established. This canon was at last committed to writing during the fifth and sixth centuries – the Great Avesta. Every single copy of this massive work was destroyed during the Arab, Turk and Mongol conquests.

Extensive bibliographies may be found listed in more extensive works by scholars of Zarathushtrianism; only a short bibliography is therefore given here:

Arrian, *Anabasis of Alexander*, Vol II, Loeb Classical Library

Bode and Nanavutty, *The Songs of Zarathushtra, The Gathas*, Ethical and Religious Classics of East and West, 1852

Boyce, Mary, *Zoroastrians, Their Religious Beliefs and Practices*, Routledge & Kegan Paul, London, 1979; (ed. and trans) *Zoroastrianism, Textual Sources for the Study of*, Manchester University Press, 1984

Dastur, R. E., *Zarathushtra and Zarathushtrianism in the Avesta*, Leipzig, 1906

Dhalla, M. N., *Zoroastrian Theology*, New York, 1914

Geldner, K. F. (ed), *Avesta, The Sacred Book of the Parsis*, 3 vols., Stuttgart, 1886-96, reprinted 1982. (The text of all Avestan passages is to be found in this edition.)

Haug, Martin, *Essays on the Sacred Language; Writings & Religion of the Parsis*, edited and enlarged by E. W. West, 3rd edition, Kegan Paul, Trench Trubner & Co., 1883. First published in Bombay, 1862

Jackson, A. V. W., *Zoroaster the Prophet of Ancient Iran*, New York, 1899

Kanga, K. E., Gujrati translation of the Avestan text, 3 vols., 1873-95

Sanjana, D. P., *Zarathushtra in the Gathas and in the Classics*. Translated from the German of Geiger and Windischmann

Taraporevala, I. J. S., *The Divine Songs of Zarathushtra*, Bombay, 1962;

The Gathas of Zarathushtra; Avesta Text with Gujrati and English translations, Bombay, 1962

Zaehner, R. C., *The Teachings of the Magi*, London, 1956 (reprinted, 1976)

Index